Analyzing
Qualitative
Data

Analyzing Qualitative Data (by Graham R. Gibbs) is the sixth part of *The SAGE Qualitative Research Kit*. This *Kit* comprises eight books and taken together the *Kit* represents the most extensive and detailed introduction to the process of doing qualitative research. This book can be used in conjunction with other titles in the *Kit* as part of this overall introduction to qualitative methods but this book can equally well be used on its own as an introduction to analyzing qualitative data.

Complete list of titles in *The SAGE Qualitative Research Kit*

- Designing Qualitative Research *Uwe Flick*
- Doing Interviews *Steinar Kvale*
- Doing Ethnographic and Observational Research *Michael Angrosino*
- Doing Focus Groups *Rosaline Barbour*
- Using Visual Data in Qualitative Research *Marcus Banks*
- Analyzing Qualitative Data *Graham R. Gibbs*
- Doing Conversation, Discourse and Document Analysis *Tim Rapley*
- Managing Quality in Qualitative Research *Uwe Flick*

Members of the Editorial Advisory Board

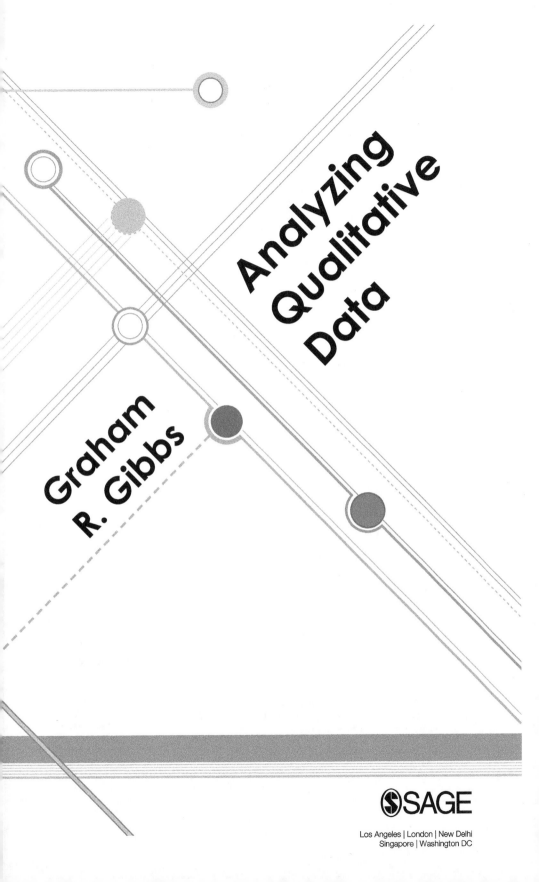

Analyzing Qualitative Data

Graham R. Gibbs

SAGE

Los Angeles | London | New Delhi
Singapore | Washington DC

First published 2007

Reprinted 2009, 2010, 2011 (twice), 2015

SAGE Publications Ltd
1 Oliver's Yard
55 City Road
London EC1Y 1SP

SAGE Publications Inc.
2455 Teller Road
Thousand Oaks, California 91320

SAGE Publications India Pvt Ltd
B 1/I 1 Mohan Cooperative Industrial Area
Mathura Road
New Delhi 110 044

SAGE Publications Asia-Pacific Pte Ltd
3 Church Street
#10-04 Samsung Hub
Singapore 049483

Library of Congress Control Number 2006938288

British Library Cataloguing in Publication data

A catalogue record for this book is available from the British Library

ISBN 978-0-7619-4980-0

Typeset by C&M Digitals (P) Ltd., Chennai, India
Printed in Great Britain by CPI Group (UK) Ltd, Croydon, CR0 4YY
Printed on paper from sustainable resources

▌▌ Contents

▐▌ List of illustrations

Boxes

Tables

Figures

Editorial introduction
Uwe Flick

- Introduction to *The SAGE Qualitative Research Kit*
- What is qualitative research?
- How do we conduct qualitative research?
- Scope of *The SAGE Qualitative Research Kit*

Introduction to *The SAGE Qualitative Research Kit*

In recent years, qualitative research has enjoyed a period of unprecedented growth and diversification as it has become an established and respected research approach across a variety of disciplines and contexts. An increasing number of students, teachers and practitioners are facing questions and problems of how to do qualitative research – in general and for their specific individual purposes. To answer these questions, and to address such practical problems on a how-to-do level, is the main purpose of *The SAGE Qualitative Research Kit*.

The books in *The SAGE Qualitative Research Kit* collectively address the core issues that arise when we actually do qualitative research. Each book focuses on key methods (e.g. interviews or focus groups) or materials (e.g. visual data or discourse) that are used for studying the social world in qualitative terms. Moreover, the books in the *Kit* have been written with the needs of many different types of reader in mind. As such, the *Kit* and the individual books will be of use to a wide variety of users:

- *Practitioners* of qualitative research in the social sciences, medical research, marketing research, evaluation, organizational, business and management studies, cognitive science, etc., who face the problem of planning and conducting a specific study using qualitative methods.
- *University teachers* and lecturers in these fields using qualitative methods will be expected to use these series as a basis of their teaching.

- *Undergraduate and graduate students* of social sciences, nursing, education, psychology and other fields where qualitative methods are a (main) part of the university training including practical applications (e.g. for writing a thesis).

Each book in *The SAGE Qualitative Research Kit* has been written by a distinguished author with extensive experience in their field and in the practice with methods they write about. When reading the whole series of books from the beginning to the end, you will repeatedly come across some issues which are central to any sort of qualitative research – such as ethics, designing research or assessing quality. However, in each book such issues are addressed from the specific methodological angle of the authors and the approach they describe. Thus you may find different approaches to issues of quality or different suggestions of how to analyze qualitative data in the different books, which will combine to present a comprehensive picture of the field as a whole.

What is qualitative research?

It has become more and more difficult to find a common definition of qualitative research which is accepted by the majority of qualitative research approaches and researchers. Qualitative research is no longer just simply '*not* quantitative research', but has developed an identity (or maybe multiple identities) of its own.

Despite the multiplicity of approaches to qualitative research, some common features of qualitative research can be identified. Qualitative research is intended to approach the world 'out there' (not in specialized research settings such as laboratories) and to understand, describe and sometimes explain social phenomena 'from the inside' in a number of different ways:

- By analyzing experiences of individuals or groups. Experiences can be related to biographical life histories or to (everyday or professional) practices; they may be addressed by analyzing everyday knowledge, accounts and stories.
- By analyzing interactions and communications in the making. This can be based on observing or recording practices of interacting and communicating and analyzing this material.
- By analyzing documents (texts, images, film or music) or similar traces of experiences or interactions.

Common to such approaches is that they seek to unpick how people construct the world around them, what they are doing or what is happening to them in terms that are meaningful and that offer rich insight. Interactions and documents are seen as ways of constituting social processes and artefacts collaboratively (or conflictingly). All of these approaches represent ways of meaning, which can be reconstructed and analyzed with different qualitative methods that allow the researcher to develop (more or less generalizable) models, typologies, theories as ways of describing and explaining social (or psychological) issues.

How do we conduct qualitative research?

Can we identify common ways of doing qualitative research if we take into account that there are different theoretical, epistemological and methodological approaches to qualitative research and that the issues that are studied are very diverse as well? We can at least identify some common features of how qualitative research is done.

- Qualitative researchers are interested in accessing experiences, interactions and documents in their natural context and in a way that gives room to the particularities of them and the materials in which they are studied.
- Qualitative research refrains from setting up a well-defined concept of what is studied and from formulating hypotheses in the beginning in order to test them. Rather, concepts (or hypotheses, if they are used) are developed and refined in the process of research.
- Qualitative research starts from the idea that methods and theories should be appropriate to what is studied. If the existing methods do not fit to a concrete issue or field, they are adapted or new methods or approaches are developed.
- Researchers themselves are an important part of the research process, either in terms of their own personal presence as researchers, or in terms of their experiences in the field and with the reflexivity they bring to the role – as are members of the field under study.
- Qualitative research takes context and cases seriously for understanding an issue under study. A lot of qualitative research is based on case studies or a series of case studies, and often the case (its history and complexity) is an important context for understanding what is studied.
- A major part of qualitative research is based on text and writing – from field notes and transcripts to descriptions and interpretations and finally to the presentation of the findings and of the research as a whole. Therefore, issues of transforming complex social situations (or other materials such as images) into texts – issues of transcribing and writing in general – are major concerns of qualitative research.
- If methods are supposed to be adequate to what is under study, approaches to defining and assessing the quality of qualitative research (still) have to be discussed in specific ways that are appropriate for qualitative research and even for specific approaches in qualitative research.

Scope of *The SAGE Qualitative Research Kit*

- *Designing Qualitative Research* (Uwe Flick) gives a brief introduction to qualitative research from the point of view of how to plan and design a concrete study using qualitative research in one way or the other. It is intended to outline a framework for the other books in *The Sage Qualitative Research Kit* by focusing on how-to-do problems and on how to solve such problems in the research process. The book will address issues of constructing a research design in qualitative research; it will outline stepping-stones in making a research project work and will discuss practical problems such as resources in qualitative research but also more methodological issues like quality of qualitative research and also ethics. This framework is spelled out in more details in the other books in the *Kit*.
- Three books are devoted to collecting or producing data in qualitative research. They take up the issues briefly outlined in the first book and approach them in a much more detailed and focused way for the specific method. First, *Doing Interviews* (Steinar Kvale) addresses the theoretical, epistemological, ethical and practical issues of interviewing people about specific issues or their life history. *Doing Ethnographic and Observational Research* (Michael Angrosino) focuses on the second major approach to collecting and producing qualitative data. Here again practical issues (like selecting sites, methods of collecting data in ethnography, special problems of analyzing them) are discussed in the context of more general issues (ethics, representations, quality and adequacy of ethnography as an approach). In *Doing Focus Groups* (Rosaline Barbour) the third of the most important qualitative methods of producing data is presented. Here again we find a strong focus on how-to-do issues of sampling, designing and analyzing the data and on how to produce them in focus groups.
- Three further volumes are devoted to analyzing specific types of qualitative data. *Using Visual Data in Qualitative Research* (Marcus Banks) extends the focus to the third type of qualitative data (beyond verbal data coming from interviews and focus groups and observational data). The use of visual data has not only become a major trend in social research in general, but confronts researchers with new practical problems in using them and analyzing them and produces new ethical issues. In *Analyzing Qualitative Data* (Graham R. Gibbs), several practical approaches and issues of making sense of any sort of qualitative data are addressed. Special attention is paid to practices of coding, of comparing and of using computer-assisted qualitative data analysis. Here, the focus is on verbal data like interviews, focus groups or biographies. *Doing Conversation, Discourse and Document Analysis* (Tim Rapley) extends this focus to different types of data, relevant for analyzing discourses. Here, the focus is on existing material (like documents) and on recording everyday

conversations and on finding traces of discourses. Practical issues such as generating an archive, transcribing video materials and of how to analyze discourses with such types of data are discussed.

- *Managing the Quality of Qualitative Research* (Uwe Flick) takes up the issue of quality in qualitative research, which has been briefly addressed in specific contexts in other books in the *Kit*, in a more general way. Here, quality is looked at from the angle of using or reformulating existing or defining new criteria for qualitative research. This book will examine the ongoing debates about what should count as defining 'quality' and validity in qualitative methodologies and will examine the many strategies for promoting and managing quality in qualitative research. Special attention is paid to the strategy of triangulation in qualitative research and to the use of quantitative research in the context of promoting the quality of qualitative research.

Before I go on to outline the focus of this book and its role in the *Kit*, I would like to thank some people at SAGE who were important in making this *Kit* happen. Michael Carmichael suggested this project to me some time ago and was very helpful with his suggestions in the beginning. Patrick Brindle took over and continued this support, as did Vanessa Harwood and Jeremy Toynboe in making books out of the manuscripts we provided.

About this book
Uwe Flick

Sometimes, analyzing qualitative data is seen as the core of qualitative research in general, whereas the collection of data is more the preliminary step in preparing this. There are different approaches to analyzing data in qualitative research, some of them more general, others more specific for certain types of data. They all have in common that they are based on textual analysis, so that any sort of material in qualitative research has to be prepared for being analyzed as text. In some cases, the internal structure of a text (for example as a narrative) is more important for the analysis than in other cases (as in a semi-structured interview). In some cases the content is at the centre of the analysis (sometimes exclusively), in other cases the interaction in the text is relevant as well (as in focus groups) or the central focus of the analysis (as in conversation analysis).

In this book, the basic analytic strategies of analyzing qualitative data are unfolded in greater detail. Its first focus is on coding and categorizing. Its second focus is on narratives and biographies. A third focus is on the use of computers in this context. Considerable attention is paid to comparative analysis and to issues of quality and ethics specific to analyzing data.

With these focuses, this book first of all provides a basis for analyzing all sorts of qualitative data of interest in verbal data, such as statements and stories. In the context of *The SAGE Qualitative Research Kit*, it is complemented by the book by Rapley (2007), which is more about the analysis of interactions – conversations in particular – and by that of Banks (2007), which addresses the analysis of visual materials. It is also complemented by the chapters in the books on ethnography by Angrosino (2007), on interviews by Kvale (2007) and on focus groups by Barbour (2007), which address particular problems of analyzing the data resulting from each method. A major addition to their scope is that this book pays much attention to using computers in qualitative research and on writing in the context of making up data (such as writing notes or memos and research diaries). It also gives helpful suggestions for transcriptions of verbal data. Its suggestions referring to ethics and quality of analysis are an addition to the books by Flick (2007a, 2007b) on design and managing quality in the research process in *The SAGE Qualitative Research Kit*.

1
The nature of qualitative analysis

Chapter objectives
After reading this chapter, you should

- see that there are some features of qualitative analysis that are distinctive, but at the same time they are features over which there is often disagreement between qualitative researchers;
- know some of the different understandings of qualitative research; and
- understand that they bear upon analysis and map out the limits of the qualitative 'territory' and some of the distinctive styles that qualitative analysts adopt.

Analysis

The idea of analysis implies some kind of transformation. You start with some (often voluminous) collection of qualitative data and then you process it, through analytic procedures, into a clear, understandable, insightful, trustworthy and even original analysis. There is disagreement even about this transformation. Some researchers focus on the 'office' processes involved – the sorting, retrieving, indexing and handling of qualitative data, usually with some discussion of how these processes can be used to generate analytic ideas (Miles and Huberman, 1994; Maykut and Morehouse, 2001; Ritchie and Lewis, 2003). The processes are designed to deal with the sheer amount of data that is created in qualitative research, in interview transcripts (see Kvale, 2007), field notes (see Angrosino,

2007), collected documents, video and audio recordings (see Rapley, 2007), and so on. Sorting and searching through all these data while at the same time creating a consistent and perceptive analysis that remains grounded in those data – that is, the data provide good supporting evidence – is a major headache. It requires good organization and a structured approach to the data. This is one of the reasons why CAQDAS, computer-assisted qualitative data analysis, has become so popular. The software does not do the thinking for you, but it helps enormously with these 'office' processes.

Other researchers emphasize the idea that analysis involves interpretation and retelling and that it is imaginative and speculative (Mishler, 1986; Riessman, 1993; Denzin, 1997; Giorgi and Giorgi, 2003). There is a range of approaches involved here, including conversation and discourse analysis (see Rapley, 2007), some forms of phenomenology, biographical and narrative approaches, as well as recent ethnographic methods (see Angrosino, 2007). These approaches emphasize the idea that qualitative data are meaningful and need to be interpreted in analysis not just to reveal the range of subject matter people are talking about but also to recognize and analyze the ways in which they frame and mould their communications.

Most writers about qualitative data analysis recognize that it involves both these aspects of analysis – data handling and interpretation (Coffey and Atkinson, 1996; Mason, 2002; Flick, 2006, 2007a). Sometimes they are used simultaneously, but often they are used in sequence starting with the use of the 'office' procedures, then moving to the reduction of data into summaries or displays, before finishing with interpretive analysis and drawing conclusions.

Qualitative data

As I have suggested above, qualitative data are essentially meaningful, but aside from that they show a great diversity. They do not include counts and measures, but they do include just about any form of human communication – written, audio or visual – behaviour, symbolism or cultural artefacts. This includes any of the following:

- individual and focus group interviews and their transcripts
- ethnographic participant observation
- e-mail
- web pages
- advertisements: printed, film or TV
- video recordings of TV broadcasts
- video diaries
- videos of interviews and focus groups

- various documents such as books and magazines
- diaries
- online chat group conversations
- online news libraries
- still photos
- film
- home videos
- video recordings of laboratory sessions

The most common form of qualitative data used in analysis is text; this can either be a transcription from interviews or field notes from ethnographic work or other kinds of documents. Most audio and video data are transformed into text to be analyzed. The reason for this is that text is any easy form of recording that can be dealt with using the 'office' techniques mentioned above. However, with the development of digital audio and video recordings and the availability of software to sort, index and retrieve it, the need and desire to transcribe might be reduced in the future. Moreover, using video data preserves some of the visual aspects of the data that are often lost when conversations are transcribed.

Practicalities of qualitative analysis

Qualitative analysis involves two activities: first, developing an awareness of the kinds of data that can be examined and how they can be described and explained; and second, a number of practical activities that assist with the kinds of data and the large amounts of it that need to be examined. The latter are what I refer to as the practicalities of qualitative analysis. I will discuss these more fully in the rest of the book, but two of them distinguish qualitative analysis from other approaches.

Merging collection and analysis

In some kinds of social research you are encouraged to collect all your data before you start any kind of analysis. Qualitative research is different from this because there is no separation of data collection and data analysis. Analysis can, and should, start in the field. As you collect your data by interviewing, taking field notes, acquiring documents, and so on, you can start your analysis. I examine these issues in more detail in Chapter 3, but things like keeping field notes and a research diary are was both to collect data and to begin its analysis. You do not even need to wait until your first interviews or field trips to start analysis. There are often plenty of data you can examine, in existing documents as well as in previous studies.

In fact, not only is concurrent analysis and data collection possible, but it can actually be good practice too. You should use the analysis of your early data as a way of raising new research issues and questions. To that extent qualitative research is flexible. Research questions can be decided late in the study, for instance, if the original questions make little sense in the light of the perspectives of those you have studied.

Expanding the volume of data, not reducing it

A further key difference between the procedures of qualitative and quantitative analysis is that the former does not seek to reduce or condense the data, for example, to summaries or to statistics. Qualitative data analysis often involves dealing with large volumes of data (transcripts, recordings, notes, etc.). Most analysis simply adds to this volume, even though at the final stage of reporting about the research, the analyst may have to select summaries and examples from the data.

Thus qualitative analysis usually seeks to enhance the data, to increase its bulk, density and complexity. In particular, many of the analytic approaches involve creating more texts in the form of things like summaries, précis, memos, notes and drafts. Many of the techniques of qualitative analysis are concerned with ways to deal with this large volume of data. This is particularly the case with coding. Whereas coding in quantitative analysis is for the explicit purpose of reducing the data to a few 'types' in order that they can be counted, coding in qualitative analysis is a way of organizing or managing the data. All the original data are preserved. Codes (and their associated analytic documents) add interpretation and theory to the data. In fact, typically, text may be densely coded; not only will most text be assigned a code, but much will have more than one code attached to it.

Methodology

The second activity that qualitative analysis involves is an awareness of the kinds of things that can be found in qualitative data and how they can be analyzed. There is a wide range of these ways of looking at the data and qualitative analysts have adopted a variety of methodologically based analytic styles to do so. Consequently there are still various contested views about methodology.

Rich description

A major concern of qualitative analysis is to describe what is happening, to answer the question 'What is going on here?' This is because very often what is described is novel or at least forgotten or ignored. The description is detailed and contributes to an understanding and eventual analysis of the setting studied. In particular, the focus is on giving a 'thick' description, a term popularized by Geertz (1975; see Mason, 2002). This is one that demonstrates the richness of what is happening and emphasizes the way that it involves people's intentions and strategies. From such a 'thick' description it is possible to go one stage further and offer an explanation for what is happening.

Induction and deduction

One of the functions of qualitative analysis is to find patterns and produce explanations. There are two contrasting logics of explanation, induction and deduction, and qualitative research actually uses both.

- *Induction* is the generation and justification of a general explanation based on the accumulation of lots of particular, but similar, circumstances. Thus, repeated, particular observations that fans of football clubs that are doing well or fans of those doing very badly are more ardent supporters than those of clubs that languish in the middle of their league sustain the general statement that the fervour of fans' support is greatest when their clubs are at the extremes of success.

• *Deductive explanation* moves in the opposite direction, in that a particular situation is explained by deduction from a general statement about the circumstances. For example, we know that as people get older their reaction times slow down, so we could deduce that Jennifer's reaction times are slow because she is over 80 years old. Much quantitative research is deductive in approach. A hypothesis is deduced from a general law and this is tested against reality by looking for circumstances that confirm or disconfirm it.

A lot of qualitative research explicitly tries to generate new theory and new explanations. In that sense the underlying logic is inductive. Rather than starting with some theories and concepts that are to be tested or examined, such research favours an approach in which they are developed in tandem with data collection in order to produce and justify new generalizations and thus create new knowledge and understanding. Some writers reject the imposition of any a priori theoretical frameworks at the outset. However, it is very hard for analysts to eliminate completely all prior frameworks. Inevitably qualitative analysis is guided and framed by pre-existing ideas and concepts. Often what researchers are doing is checking hunches; that is, they are deducing particular explanations from general theories and seeing if the circumstances they observe actually correspond.

Nomothetic and idiographic

Both inductive and deductive approaches are concerned with general statements, but much qualitative research examines the particular, the distinctive or even unique.

• The *nomothetic* approach takes an interest in the general dimensions on which all individuals and situations vary. The approach assumes that the behaviour of a particular person is the outcome of laws that apply to all. To put it less formally, the approach tries to show what people, events and settings have in common and to explain them in terms of these common features. In qualitative research this is done by looking for variations and differences and trying to relate or even correlate them with other observed features like behaviours, actions and outcomes.
• The *idiographic* approach studies the individual (person, place, event, setting, etc.) as a unique case. The focus is on the interplay of factors that might be quite specific to the individual. Even though two individuals might share some aspects in common, these will inevitably be materially affected by other differences between them. Thus two heterosexual couples may have a lot in

common: same ages, same culture, same number of children and similar houses in the same location. But there will be many differences too. They may have different jobs, have come from different social backgrounds, have different interests, and their children may have different personalities and different relationships with their parents. A qualitative study of the couples would have to recognize that their commonalities would be crucially shaped by their differences so that each couple could be seen as unique.

In qualitative research there is a strong emphasis on exploring the nature of a particular phenomenon. The concern with the idiographic is often manifest in the examination of case studies. Such an approach stresses not only the uniqueness of each case, but also the holistic nature of social reality. That is to say, factors and characteristics can only be properly understood by reference to the wider context of other factors and features.

Both the nomothetic and idiographic approaches are common in qualitative research. The idiographic is often seen as a specific strength of qualitative research, and is particularly associated with certain analytic techniques such as biography and narrative. However, the combining and contrasting of several cases often provides the analyst with the warrant for making nomothetic claims too.

Realism and constructivism

Qualitative researchers also disagree about the reality of the world they are trying to analyze. In particular they disagree about whether there is a material world that has characteristics that exist independently of us and which acts as an ultimate reference for the validity of our analysis.

- *Realism.* This is probably the everyday assumption of most people as they go about their lives. Those who are realists believe that in some sense there is a world with a character and structure that exists apart from us and our lives. At the most basic, and probably least controversial, this is the view that there is a material world of objects that existed before we did and would continue to exist even if we all perished. This is the world of physical objects, landscape, animals and plants, planets and stars and all the things that can be seen, felt, heard, tasted and smelt. The realist view gets more controversial when we start to think about things that are more theoretical and that cannot be directly sensed. These include some of the more abstract ideas of physics and mathematics, such as atoms, weak nuclear forces, neutrinos, probabilities and imaginary numbers, as well as the things that qualitative researchers might discuss, like social class, political power, learning styles, attitudes, reference groups, social mores and state laws. For a realist, such things are real and independent of us, and even if they cannot be directly seen or felt, their effects can. There is only one way the world is. Our descriptions and explanations of it are to varying

6

degrees accurate portrayals of that world and are correct to the extent that they correspond with this real world.

- *Idealism/constructivism.* In contrast, idealists suggest that we actually cannot know anything about such a real world. Everything we say and experience is through the medium of our constructs and ideas. Even the very idea of reality itself is a human construct. The world we experience reflects these concepts and consequently if they are different or change, then the world is different too. People used to believe witches had supernatural powers and that the Earth was flat. Now very few believe either and consequently the world for us is different. Constructivism is a version of idealism which stresses that the world we experience arises from multiple, socially constructed realities. These constructions are created because individuals want to make sense of their experiences. Very often they are shared, but that 'does not make them more real, but simply more commonly assented to' (Guba and Lincoln, 1989, p. 89). Thus a constructivist analysis tries to reflect as faithfully as possible the constructions without any reference to an underlying or shared reality. Some statements might appear to be objective descriptions of reality, but inevitably they are 'theory-laden' and reflect our preconceptions and prejudices arising from our and/or our respondents' constructions of the world. For idealists and constructivists, we cannot say how the world is, only how some people see it. This view might seem easy to support when talking about people's accounts or stories about events. It is very easy to see how these might be partial and biased and reflect their constructions of the world. But for a constructivist this applies equally to what might be claimed as objective data, such as direct observation of people's behaviour. These data, for the constructivist, equally reflect the interplay of the researcher's and the participant's constructions.

In practice, few qualitative analysts are purely realist or idealist. Most are concerned to portray, as accurately and faithfully as possible, what people actually said and to that extent they are realists. However, all would agree that qualitative research is a matter of interpretation, especially the researcher's interpretation of what respondents and participants say and do. A key commitment of qualitative research is to see things through the eyes of respondents and participants. This involves a commitment to viewing events, actions, norms, values, and so on from the perspective of those being studied. The researcher needs to be sensitive to the differing perspectives held by different groups and to the potential conflict between the perspective of those being studied and those doing the studying. Thus, there can be no simple, true and accurate reporting of respondents' views. Our analyses are themselves interpretations and thus constructions of the world.

Ethics

Ethical issues bear upon qualitative research like any other research. However, they mostly affect the stages of planning and data collection. For example, the principle of fully informed consent means that participants in research should know exactly what they are letting themselves in for, what will happen to them during the research, and what will happen to the data they provide after the research is completed. They should be made aware of this before research on them starts and they should be given the option to withdraw from the research at any time and usually, if they request it, any data that have been collected from them will be returned or destroyed. All of this happens well before the data are analyzed.

However, there are some special aspects of qualitative data and their collection that raise ethical issues. Perhaps the most significant is that qualitative data are usually very personal and individual. The identification of individuals cannot be hidden behind aggregated statistics when data are analyzed and reported on. Unless special steps are taken, reporting on qualitative data, and especially the use of direct quotations from respondents, will commonly identify specific participants and/or settings. Sometimes this is not an issue, and especially when it is with the agreement of participants, their real identity and that of the settings and organizations they are operating in can be revealed. But usually this is not the case. We are normally required to go to some lengths to protect the identity of those involved in our research. Chapter 2 discusses some of the aspects of anonymization of transcripts that are required in qualitative analysis.

The personal nature of much qualitative research means that researchers need to be very sensitive to the possible harm and upset their work might cause to participants. Again, mostly these issues arise at the stage of data collection, when, for example, the nature of depth interviews might allow people to talk at length and in depth about issues they would not normally address. Researchers have to be aware of the distress this might cause participants and make provisions for dealing with it. By the time the data are analyzed, these issues should have been dealt with, although there might still be some remaining issues connected with the publication of the results of the analysis. These issues will be discussed further in Chapter 7.

Key points

- Qualitative data are very varied, but all have in common that they are examples of human meaningful communication. For reasons of convenience most such data are converted to written (or typed) text. The analysis of what is often a large amount of material reflects two characteristics. First, the data are voluminous and there need to be methods for dealing with this in a practical and consistent way. Second, the data need to be interpreted.

- There are some practical issues that make qualitative data analysis distinctive. These include starting data analysis before the sampling is decided and the data collection is complete, and the fact that the analysis of the data tends to increase its volume (at least to start with) rather than reduce it.

- There is a tendency to see qualitative research as constructionist, inductive and idiographic. That is to say, to see it as concerned with the interpretation of new explanations about the unique features of individual cases. However, this is a gross simplification. Much qualitative research is concerned with explaining what people and situations have in common and doing this with reference to existing theories and concepts. To that extent it is nomothetic and deductive. In addition, although all researchers are sensitive to the way that even their descriptions are interpretations, they are sufficiently realist to believe that it is important to represent the views of participants and respondents as faithfully and accurately as possible.
- Because of its individual and personal nature, qualitative research raises a host of ethical issues. However, most of these should have been dealt with before data analysis starts. Nevertheless, it is important to ensure that anonymity is preserved (if the assurance has been given) and that respondents know what will happen to the data they have provided.

Further reading

The following works will extend the issues of this brief introduction in more detail:

Angrosino, M. (2007). *Doing Ethnographic and Observational Research* (Book 3 of *The SAGE Qualitative Research Kit*). London: Sage.

Barbour, R. (2007) *Doing Focus Groups* (Book 4 of *The SAGE Qualitative Research Kit*). London: Sage.

Crotty, M. (1998) *The Foundations of Social Research: Meaning and Perspective in the Research Process*. London: Sage.

Flick, U. (2007a) *Designing Qualitative Research* (Book 1 of *The SAGE Qualitative Research Kit*). London: Sage.

Flick, U., von Kardorff, E. and Steinke, I. (eds) (2004) *A Companion to Qualitative Research*. London: Sage. See especially parts 3A and 4.

Hesse-Biber, S.N. and Leavy, P. (eds) (2004) *Approaches to Qualitative Research: A Reader on Theory and Practice*. New York: Oxford University Press. See especially part I.

Kvale, S. (2007) *Doing Interviews* (Book 2 of *The SAGE Qualitative Research Kit*). London: Sage.

Rapley, T. (2007) *Doing Conversation, Discourse and Document Analysis* (Book 7 of *The SAGE Qualitative Research Kit*). London: Sage.

2
Data preparation

Chapter objectives
After reading this chapter, you should

- know that most analysts work with textual data, usually neatly transcribed and typed;
- see that the task of transcription is time-consuming and must be
  done carefully and with pre-planning as it involves a change of
  medium and thus inevitably a degree of interpretation; and
- be aware of the decisions to be made about the process and level of
  transcription, naming conventions, anonymization and formatting.

Transcription

Most qualitative researchers transcribe their interview recordings, observations
and field notes to produce a neat, typed copy. However, there are two big issues
to bear in mind before undertaking transcriptions: they take a lot of time and
effort to do and transcription is an interpretive process. Estimates of the time
transcripts take vary from author to author and depend on what level of detail you
transcribe and how talented the typist is. A common figure is that transcribing
takes somewhere between 4 and 6 times as long as it takes to collect the data.
This means that work can pile up, especially for the lone researcher doing their
own transcription. Many PhD students using qualitative methods have
experienced the anxiety brought on in the later stages of their fieldwork by the
growing 'pile' of tapes and notes waiting to be transcribed. The only real advice

here, albeit hard to follow, is, if you can't pay someone to do it for you, keep transcribing 'little and often'.

Transcription, especially of interviews, is a change of medium and that introduces issues of accuracy, fidelity and interpretation. Kvale (1988, p. 97) warns us to 'beware of transcripts'. There are, he suggests, dangers when moving from the spoken context of an interview to the typed transcript, such as superficial coding, decontextualization, missing what came before and after the respondent's account, and missing what the larger conversation was about. As we shall see later, this change of medium is associated with certain kinds of errors that researchers must watch out for. One corrective here is to go back to the recording to check your interpretations based on the transcript. You may find that hearing the voice makes the meaning clearer and even suggests different interpretations. Furthermore, most transcripts only capture the spoken aspects of the interview and miss out the setting, context, body language and general 'feel' of the session. Mishler (1991) suggests a parallel between a transcript and a photograph. A photograph is one, frozen, framed, printed and edited version of reality. The same is true of a transcript. The issue is not whether the transcript is, in a final sense, accurate, but rather whether it represents a good, careful attempt to capture some aspects of the interview. There is always an issue of how to convert speech into written text. Very few people speak in grammatical prose, so the researcher needs to decide how much of what is in the recording needs to be transcribed. As we shall see later there are several options here, although we have to recognize that the transcript will never be completely accurate.

A similar point can be made about the move from handwritten notes taken during interviews or during fieldwork. Transcription here usually involves a process of 'writing up' the notes. This is a creative activity and not just a mechanical reproduction. It involves expressing the notes as ideas, observations of certain kinds and so on, and represents the start of data analysis as well. I will discuss these issues in more detail in the next chapter.

Reasons for transcribing

It is not necessary to transcribe all or even any of the information you have collected in your project in order to analyze it. Some levels and forms of analysis can be done quite productively without any copy of the interviews, texts or observations you have collected or recorded. In fact some researchers advocate analyzing directly from a tape or video recording. That way you are more likely to focus on the bigger picture and not get bogged down in the details of what people have said. This is fine for some types of analysis, but for others, such as discourse and conversation analysis, a detailed transcript is a necessity. It forces you to read carefully what was recorded on tape or in your notes and it provides you with an easily readable version that can be copied as many times as necessary. Having a transcript also makes it easier to work in a team, where tasks have to be shared and there has to be good agreement about the interpretation of the data. A type-script means everyone can read the texts and everyone can have a copy.

Strategies for transcribing interviews

There are various strategies you can adopt when transcribing. You could, for example, only transcribe parts of the recording. For the rest, you could just take notes and use those for coding and analysis, or even code directly from the tape or handwritten notes. In some cases you may find that your memory of an interview or your research diary tells you that at certain points the respondent went off topic and so these parts can be ignored. Such an approach will clearly be quicker, and might also allow you to focus on the larger themes and not get bogged down in the particular words. But there are several drawbacks. You may find that the parts you have transcribed lose their context and you find it harder to interpret what they really mean. Moreover the ideas you have at the start of analysis, which might lead you to decide what parts need transcribing, may well be different from those you develop later in the study.

Names

The convention is to put the name of the person interviewed, in capitals, at the start of each speech (i.e. each answer to the interviewer's questions). Putting the name in capitals makes it stand out on the page but also means you can use case-sensitive search and find to look for what the interviewee said only or just when their name is used elsewhere in the interviews. This is particularly useful when analysing focus group discussions. Use the name that is easiest for you to remember the interviewees by. This is usually their first name. Then either type colon, tab before the actual text, or start the text on a new line. If you are dealing with a large number of interviews then you might opt to indicate the person's sur-name with their first name and surname (or first letter of surname), as in 'MARY C:' to distinguish them from others with the same first name. Indicate the interviewer's speech in the same way. Use 'I:' or 'IV:' or 'INT:' at the start, or if you have several interviewers and you want to distinguish them in the transcripts, then use 'I-JOHN:', 'I-KATE:', and so on. Make sure that all names are spelled correctly and consistently. This means you can use search and find in your word processor to anonymize the text and find all the speech by the same person in CAQDAS programs.

Anonymization

As you will eventually be quoting from your transcripts in your write-up of the research and you might even be depositing the data in a public archive so that other researchers have access to it, you will need to consider how you will ensure confidentiality. Do this by anonymizing the names of people and places to make it safe for participants (if their activities are illegal or illicit) and safe for the researcher (e.g. if you have been investigating covert operations or paramilitary groups). It is easiest to produce an anonymized copy immediately after transcription. However, you may find it is best to do your analysis using the unanonymized version as familiarity with the real names and places can make it easier.

Create a listing, in a separate file, kept somewhere safe, of all the names – people, places, organizations, companies, products – that you have changed and what you have substituted. Use search and find in your word processor to find each name and substitute it with the anonymized version. Make sure you search for both normal text versions of respondent's names ('Mary') if these appear in other respondent's interviews as well as capitalized versions ('MARY:') if you have used that to identify speakers. It is usually best to use pseudonyms rather than crude blanks, asterisks, code numbers, and so on. You will still need to read the transcript carefully to ensure that more subtle, but obvious clues to a person, place or institution are not evident. If you are going to deposit your data into a data archive, then remember you will need to retain and deposit the original, unanonymized versions alongside the accessible anonymized versions.

Box 2.1   Conversational features

- **Abbreviations** (e.g. isn't, aren't, weren't, could've, I'd, she's, he'd, I'm, you're, they've, we'll, don't, haven't, that's, 'cause, something's, who's) sometimes spelled out by transcribers.
- **Verbal tics**, like 'er', 'um', 'erm'. Often ignored, but others such as 'like', 'y'know' and 'sort of' usually get included.
- **Pauses**. Either cut or shown simply by three dots (...).
- **Repetitions** (for example, 'What I mean ... I mean ... what I want to says is ... I mean that is a real problem') might simply be rendered as 'That is a real problem'.

Adapted from Arksey and Knight (1999, p. 146).

Level of transcription

I noted above that the act of transcription is a change of medium and therefore necessarily involves a transformation of the data. There are varying degrees to which you can capture what is in the sound recording (or your handwritten notes) and you need to decide what is appropriate for the purposes of your study. Sometimes just a draft version of what is said is sufficient. This is often the case in policy, organization and evaluation research, where the salient factual content of what people have said is good enough for analysis. However, most researchers who are interested at least in respondents' interpretation of their world need more detail than this. They aim at a transcribed text that looks like normal text and is a good copy of the words that were used. This may seem straightforward, but even here there are decisions to be made. Continuous speech is very rarely in well-constructed sentences. Speakers stop one line of thought in mid-sentence and often take up the old one again without following the grammatical rules used in writing. And there are all kinds of features that aren't often captured by written prose (see Box 2.1).

You may therefore be tempted to 'tidy up' their speech. Whether you should do this depends on the purpose of your study. Tidy, grammatical transcripts are easier to read and hence analyze. If your study is not much concerned with the details of expression and language use and is more interested in the factual content of what is said, then such tidying up is acceptable. On the other hand, it clearly loses the feel for how respondents were expressing themselves and if that is significant in your study, you will need to try and capture that in the transcription. The downside is that it makes the actual typing more difficult to do. A similar dilemma arises when respondents speak with a strong accent or use dialect. The most common practice here is to preserve all the dialect words and regional terms and grammatical expressions, but not to try to capture the actual sound of the accent by changing the spelling of the words. Keeping to a standard and consistent spelling is important if you are going to use the search functions in software to help with the analysis (see Chapter 9). It is harder to find all the text you are looking for if you haven't spelled terms consistently. This is important if you are going to use computer seaching. Box 2.2 gives some examples of different transcription styles.

Box 2.2   Examples of different levels of transcription

Just the gist

'90% of my communication is with ... the Sales Director. 1% of his communication is with me. I try to be one step ahead, I get things ready, ... because he jumps from one ... project to another. ... This morning we did Essex, this afternoon we did BT, and we haven't even finished Essex yet.'
(... indicates omitted speech)

Verbatim

'I don't really know. I've a feeling that they're allowed to let their emotions show better. I think bereavement is part of their religion and culture. They tend to be more religious anyway. I'm not from a religious family, so I don't know that side of it.'

(Continued)

(Continued)

Verbatim with dialect

'Well ... first time I were with ... I was still at school, I were fifteen ... an' ... me brother 'ad gone into army ... and me mum and dad said that it wasn't workin' out, me livin' at 'ome ... an' ... I don't know ... really I don't why they kicked me out, but they did and I ended up livin' with me cousin.'

Discourse level

Bashir: Did your ever (.) personally assist him with the writing of his book. (0.8)
Princess: A lot of people.hhh ((clears throat)) saw the distress that my life was in. (.) And they felt it was a supportive thing to help (0.2) in the way that they did.

From Silverman (1997, p. 151).

In some cases, for example if you are undertaking a discourse analysis or a conversation analysis, an even more detailed transcription is necessary. Not only is natural speech often non-grammatical (at least by written conventions), but it is also full of other phenomena. People hesitate, they stress words and syllables, they overlap their speech with others and they raise and lower both volume and pitch in order to add meaning to what they are saying. If you need to record these features then there are various transcription conventions you can follow. One of the most widely used is the Jefferson system (see Atkinson and Heritage, 1984) and a similar system can be found in Silverman (1997, p. 254; see also Rapley, 2007; Kvale, 2007).

Doing the transcription

The researcher

The choice of who should do the transcription usually comes down to either you, the researcher, or someone else who is paid to do it. Despite the nature of the activity, which can be tedious especially if you are not a good touch typist, there are advantages to doing your own transcription. It gives you a chance to start the data analysis. Careful listening to tapes and reading and checking of the transcript you have produced means that you become very familiar with the content. Inevitably you start to generate new ideas about the data. Nevertheless, researchers usually do their own transcription because they have no choice. They have no funds to employ an audiotypist or the content of the recording means that no one else can do it. For instance, the interviews may be about a highly technical subject or, what

15

is often the case with anthropological work, in a language very few others can understand.

If you are transcribing tapes yourself, try if at all possible to use a proper transcription machine. This is a tape player that can play normal audiocassettes, not mini-tapes of the kind used in dictation machines, as qualitative researchers usually use audiocassettes for taping interviews. Transcription machines have two facilities that make them superior to an audiocassette player. They have a foot control that allows you to pause the tape without using your hands. This is very useful if you are a touch typist. Second, when the play is restarted after a pause, the tape has rewound a little and starts a little before the place where you paused. Typically the length of rewind can be adjusted to match your speed and accuracy of typing and how difficult it is to make out what is on the tape. If you use an ordinary audiocassette player you will find yourself constantly frustrated by having to rewind the tape a little each time you stop. You can replace the transcription machine with software if you go digital (See Box 2.3).

Box 2.3 Digital recordings

A recent alternative to using a transcription machine is digitizing the recording (usually to MP3 format) and then playing the recording on the computer while you transcribe. There is some good, free software that will enable you to control the playing as you type. For example, one program allows you to type into a text box as you hear the tape and then pause and restart the speech using a function key. The advantage of digitization is that the pause is instantaneous and no words are lost when you restart the playing and there is little need for rewinding. Another program allows you to split the speech into short phrases that are easier to control while transcribing.

At the moment, the difficulty with this approach is digitizing the recording. You need to have the equipment that supports this – a sound card and the appropriate connectors on your computer – and the software that can digitize the recording. Moreover, the digitizing is real time. That is, one hour of recording will take one hour of computer time to digitize, although once started, you can leave the computer to it. In fact, if this approach seems attractive, you can avoid the digitization process altogether by using a digital voice recorder in the first place. Some of these are designed for taking dictation, others are for recording and playing music but have microphones too. If you use one that records in MP3 format, then you can simply download the recording directly to the computer and use the transcription software just described (otherwise you may have to convert the digital file format to MP3).

(Continued)

(Continued)

If your original source is digital video, then whilst there is no need to digitize, you may need to convert the sound to, e.g., MP3 format in order to play it in your transcription software. Another issue here is that you may want to preserve the timing links between the images and sound and the transcription. In that case you will need to use software dedicated to video analysis and/or to video transcription.

Audiotypist

Employing someone else to do the transcription, if you can afford it, is a good option, especially if the tapes are easily understandable or the notes and documents that need transcribing are easy to read. It is best if the typist you are employing knows something about the subject matter and the context of the interviews. Also make sure they know what kind of level of transcription you require. Check their work early on to make sure it is in the format you want. No matter whom you use, you will still need to check through the document produced against the recording or original text to eliminate mistakes. However, this is not all lost time as, again, reading the transcript (and listening to the tape) will be an opportunity to begin your analysis.

Don't forget that the typist will be listening to or reading all your data. As Gregory, Russell and Phillips remind us, they are 'vulnerable' persons (Gregory et al., 1997). If the content of your data is emotionally loaded and sensitive, you might want to consider including your transcribers in the scope of your ethical considerations and you may wish to offer some debriefing to support them.

OCR and speech recognition software

In recent years, two new technologies have become available that can help the transcription process. If you have some typed or printed documents that you need to get an electronic copy of, then optical character recognition (OCR) software used with a scanner will help. Provided the original paper copy is good quality and that standard fonts are used, like Courier for typescript, then the software will work well in producing word-processing files from the paper copies. Save your text as plain text because the layout, fonts, and so on that formatted text gives you are seldom of much relevance to your analysis.

A more recent technology that is sometimes used by qualitative researchers is speech recognition software. This takes speech spoken into a special, high-quality microphone and converts it into a word-processed file. The software can be used with natural speech and it can also cope with versions of English, such as UK

English, South-East Asian and Indian English, as well as a few non-English languages, such as Spanish. However, it always needs to be trained to recognize the speech of one particular user and needs very good quality sound. For these reasons it cannot be used directly with recordings of respondents and especially recordings of focus groups. However, what some enterprising researchers have done is to set up a tape player with a pair of headphones with which they can listen to the recording. Then as the tape plays they pause after each phrase and dictate into the speech recognition software, rather in the manner of a parallel translator. The accuracy can be variable, but it is generally sufficient for a first draft transcription that can then be checked against the tape properly. Speech recognition is a computationally intensive task and all programs need fairly powerful computers. Check before you buy.

Accuracy

No matter how the transcription is produced – OCR, speech recognition or human typist – it will need checking against the original. Errors arise for a variety of reasons. First there are simple typing errors, misspellings, and so on. Most of these can be picked up using the spelling checker and grammar checker built into most word processors. Nevertheless, in most cases you will want to record exactly what the respondent said, even if it is ungrammatical. Other, and often more insidious errors arise because the transcriber has misheard what was said on the tape. Sometimes this is because the recording was made in a noisy place or it has picked up the sound of the recorder mechanism and it is hard to make out what is said. In face-to-face speech humans are very good at filtering out such noises, but recordings do not and then we experience more difficulty hearing over the background. But even where the sound is good there are many cases where the transcriber has heard one thing whereas the respondent said something else. Hearing exactly what is said involves understanding and interpretation. Sometimes the right sound is heard but the interpretation is wrong, as in the UK comedian Ronnie Barker's classic comedy sketch on the confusion between 'four candles' and 'fork handles'. More often than not, though, it is in the process of interpretation that something different is heard from what was actually said. Table 2.1 lists some of the errors of interpretation found by a Canadian researcher using audio-typists to transcribe interviews on trade union activities.

Various things can be done to minimize these errors. It helps to have as good a quality sound as possible. So use good equipment. But no matter how good the sound, there is always going to be a need for interpretation and understanding of what is heard. The best way to reduce errors here is to make sure that the transcriber understands the context and subject matter he or she is transcribing and is used to the accent, cadence and rhythm of the speakers. In this sense, transcribers may need training to help them become familiar with the subject matter. This is

TABLE 2.1   Examples of transcription errors

Transcriber's typed phrase	What interviewee actually said
Random interpretations	
reflective bargaining	collective bargaining
the various	those areas
leading	relating
certain kinds of ways of understanding	surface kinds of ways of understanding
and our	and/or
generally	gender lines
mixed service	lip service
overrated	overridden
accepted committee	executive committee
denying neglect	benign neglect
Opposite meanings	
ever meant to	never meant to
it just makes sense	it doesn't make sense
there isn't a provision for day care	there is a provision for day care
formal	informal
there's one thing I can add	there's nothing I can add
there's more discernible actions	there aren't discernible factions

From e-mail from Carl Cuneo, 16 June 1994, QUALRS-L Listserv.

one of the biggest advantages of doing your own transcription. You will know the context of the interview and, I hope, be familiar with the subject matter.

You should also use your word processor to check the spellings in your text. Not only should common words be spelled correctly, but proper names and dialect and jargon terms should also be spelled consistently. This means that if you are using software to assist your analysis you can use the search facility in it without having to worry about alternative spellings.

Printing the transcript

Even if you intend to use CAQDAS for recording all your analysis, you may still want to print out your transcripts because it is easier to check them, you can show them to respondents for checking, and because you want to do some analysis on the printed copy. One thing to decide about at this stage is whether you are going to use CAQDAS for your main analysis or for keeping the definitive record of your analysis – especially your coding. If you are doing either, then you should ensure that your printouts are the same as the text that appears on screen when you have imported transcripts into your CAQDAS. That way you make it easier to transfer into the software any notes you have written on the transcripts. In this case it is best to import your transcripts into the CAQDAS and use that program to print them out.

If you do not intend to use CAQDAS then you can print directly from your word processor. There are three things to consider:

1. *Line numbers.* If you want your transcripts to show line numbers (some approaches recommend this, e.g. for cross-referencing), then use your word processor to set this up. Most have an option to do this automatically – you don't have to do it manually (e.g. in MS Word click **Format:Documents** then **Layout** tab. Click **Line Numbers** button then the **Add line numbering** check box and **Continuous** radio button. Numbers are only visible on screen in Page Layout View). N.B. If you are using CAQDAS then use that software to insert line numbers. Do not do it in your word processor before you import the files to your project.

2. *Margins.* Leave wide margins on the sheets for you to annotate and indicate coding ideas. Most people leave a wide margin on the right. Use the margin setting in your word processor (e.g. in MS Word select all the text – **Edit: Select All** – then move the margin tabs in the ruler).

3. *Line spacing.* Double-space the text (or use space and a half). Again this leaves room for underlining, comments and circling the text. (In MS Word, select all the text – **Edit:Select All** – then **Format:Paragraph** …, then **Indents and Spacing** tab. Select **1.5** or **Double** line spacing from the pop-down menu.)

Internet data

One way to avoid most of the problems associated with transcription is to collect your data via the Internet. All textual data that can be gathered from the Internet, for example, e-mail messages, web pages, chat room dialogues, commercial news archives, and so on, come already in electronic form. No transcription is required. Most e-mail is still plain text. So there is no problem just saving the messages as that. However, it is important to keep the header information too, so that you know who the message was from, whom it was to, when it was sent and what topic it was about. Some e-mails are threaded, that is, messages on the same topic are linked together chronologically. You may want to preserve the threading in your files for analysis, for example, by putting all messages in the same thread in the same file, in chronological order.

Web pages present a different problem. They are written not in plan text but in a mark-up language, HTML, so that they can be displayed in a formatted form in web browsers. They may also include various multimedia elements such as images, sounds and movies. You need to decide if you just need the text, in which case save the pages as plain text (an option in the **File: Save As …** menu), or whether you want to save them as web pages (or web archives), including the multimedia elements. Most CAQDAS programs can import and code plain text files. Very few can handle rich multimedia items such as web pages and sounds and video, and of those that do, very few support the direct coding of such items. The software you have available may limit you to analyzing the text only and you will have to examine the multimedia items in other ways. Web pages also typically contain hyperlinks to other web pages. They are therefore an excellent example of intertextuality, the linkage between and interdependence of documents. Thus it is a moot point whether the meaning of a web page is indicated just by the content of the page itself or whether you need to include some or all of the hyperlinked pages. Saving a site as a web archive may be one option, though this may not be able to deal with all the relevant hyperlinks such as those to external websites and means that it is hard to use CAQDAS.

In some cases, such as when using commercial news archives, even if you convert the files to plain text, you may need to undertake some processing and filtering to eliminate superfluous and irrelevant material. The process of selection may not be selective enough, as Seale found when he searched a commercial news archive for articles on cancer (Seale, 2002). A lot of the articles he received were about astrology and the star sign Cancer and not about the illness that he was interested in.

Metadata

Put simply, metadata is data about data. In the context of data preparation there are two important forms of metadata to consider. First there is information about your interviews, notes, and so on, that records their provenance, an outline of their content and who they involve. Second is information about the details of your data that you need for archiving, such as details of how the study was carried out and biographical information about your respondents.

Information about the provenance of a document is kept in the document summary or the cover sheet (so called because when transcripts were typewritten such data were kept on the separate, top or cover sheet of paper). If you are producing electronic transcripts (such as word processor files), then it is a simple matter to include this information at the start of your file. Typical contents are listed in Box 2.4.

Box 2.4   Typical contents of metadata documents

Document summary form or document description

Typically this would summarize information about an interview and include (as appropriate):

- Date of interview
- Biographical details about the respondent
- Topic and circumstances of interview
- Name of interviewer
- Source of field notes relevant to interview
- Linked documents (e.g. previous and subsequent interviews)
- Source of document (full reference)
- Initial ideas for analysis
- Pseudonym of person interviewed and other anonymizing references

---

Preparing for archives

In some cases you may want to deposit your data into an archive so that others can use your work and possibly reanalyze it. In the UK there is an organization, Qualidata, the ESRC Qualitative Data Archival Resource Centre, that can advise on this. Their website http://www.esds.ac.uk/qualidata/ contains detailed advice on what you need to do. As I mentioned above, you will need to anonymize the transcripts, but archives normally want to have the unanonymized originals too, along with details of how they were anonymized. Secondary users of the data are obliged to maintain anonymity as you have done. If material is particularly sensitive, you can make the material closed for a certain period or restrict access to it.

Archives normally need all the various accompanying material you used. This includes documentation such as the cover sheets just discussed and field notes and other written or printed documents you have collected along with details of your sampling strategy, your interview schedules, and so on. It may take some time and effort to get all these materials into a suitable state for deposition. If you are required to archive your data (as projects funded by the ESRC are), then allow resources for this (see Rapley, 2007).

Key points

- Most qualitative data are transcribed into typed (or word-processed) text. This is because analysts find it easier to work with typed copy than with scribbled notes, audiotape or video recordings. However, transcription involves a change of medium and therefore a degree of transformation and interpretation of the data.

- One consequence is that you will need to decide what level of transcription to use; whether you want to transcribe every pause, stress, pitch change and overlapping speech as well as every word spoken or whether a less detailed rendering is sufficient for your purpose.
- It is always best if you personally undertake the transcription, as you already know the subject matter well and are less likely to make mistakes, but also because it gives you a chance to start thinking about your analysis. There is now some new technology, such as OCR and voice recognition software, that might make the task easier. However, if you have the resources, you can pay a transcriber to do the work.
- Either way, the accuracy of the transcription is important. You need to check your own typing or check that done by your transcriber. It is very easy to make mistakes that can radically change the meaning.
- One way you can avoid a lot of transcription is to collect your data from the Internet. Data from e-mail, chat rooms, web pages, blogs and the like mean that someone else has already done the typing for you. However, you may still need to do some processing to convert the data into the form you need for your analysis or that is needed for your CAQDAS.

Further reading

The following works will extend the issues of this brief introduction in more detail.

Bird, C.M. (2005) 'How I stopped dreading and learned to love transcription', *Qualitative Inquiry*, 11(2): 226–48.

Kvale, S. (2007) *Doing Interviews* (Book 2 of *The SAGE Qualitative Research Kit*). London: Sage.

Park, J. and Zeanah, A.E. (2005) 'An evaluation of voice recognition software for use in interview-based research: a research note', *Qualitative Research*, 5(2): 245–51.

Poland, B.D. (2001) 'Transcription quality', in J.F. Gubrium and J.A. Holstein (eds), *Handbook of Interview Research: Context and Method*. Thousand Oaks, CA: Sage, pp. 629–49.

Rapley, T. (2007) *Doing Conversation, Discourse and Document Analysis* (Book 7 of *The SAGE Qualitative Research Kit*). London: Sage.

3
Writing

Chapter objectives
After reading this chapter, you should

- understand the role of writing as part of analysis;
- know the three kinds of written output that are commonly used in qualitative analysis: the research diary, field notes and memos;
- understand more about their role in furthering your analytic thinking; and
- see the need to write throughout your project so that when you undertake your final write-up you will already have written much that can simply be incorporated into it.

No matter what their methodological orientation, all writers on qualitative analysis agree about the importance of writing things down, whether this is jotting down ideas, collecting field notes or creating a report of your work. There is no substitute, throughout the whole period of analysis, for writing about the data you have collected and using writing as a way of developing ideas about what the data indicate, how they can be analyzed and what interpretations can be made. Consequently, this chapter is early in the book for two reasons:

1. It is not a good idea to leave all your writing to what is often called a 'writing-up' stage. Start writing as early as you can. Writing as you work through data collection and analysis will encourage you to set down your ideas and hunches, even though, in all likelihood, these thoughts will get extensively altered as you proceed through your project. You may be tempted to write just notes because that is all you have time for, but try to avoid leaving the ideas

as notes. Go back and 'write them up' into a narrative as soon as you can and preferably into a word processor or into your CAQDAS. Do the same with any handwritten jottings. This is because:

- Notes that make sense to you as you jot them down may not when you come back to them months, if not years, later.
- Writing is thinking. It is natural to believe that you need to be clear in your mind what you are trying to express first before you can write it down. However, most of the time the opposite is true. You may think you have a clear idea, but it is only when you write it down that you can be certain that you do (or sadly, sometimes, that you do not). Having to communicate your ideas is an excellent test of how far you have a clear understanding and how coherent your ideas are. Writing is an ideal way of doing this. See Table 3.1 for some good practice in writing.

2. In a very real sense, writing up your notes and writing the final narrative account of your work are, especially in qualitative research, central parts of the analysis itself. A lot of qualitative analysis involves interpretation. You have to work out what is going on, what things mean and why they are happening. What you start with is a lot of words, pictures, sounds or video images. These are all meaningful, but you need to interpret them and{ re-express them in a way that is both faithful to the respondents, informants and settings you are investigating, and at the same time informs and explains things to the readers of your reports.

TABLE 3.1 The two golden rules

(a) Write early and write often; (b) don't get it right, get it written.

The 'write early and write often' rule works because:

1. The more you write, the easier it gets.
2. If you write every day, it becomes a habit.
3. Tiny bits of writing add up to a lot of writing. Break the writing up into small bits. Write 100 words on X, 200 words on Y and then file them safely. It all mounts up.
4. The longer you leave it unwritten, the worse the task becomes.

The 'don't get it right, get it written' rule works because:

1. Until it is on paper no one can help you to get it right. Draft, show the draft to people, redraft.
2. Drafting is a vital stage in clarifying thought.
3. Start writing the bit that is clearest in your head: not the Introduction, but Chapter 4, or the appendices, or the conclusions, or the methods. As you draft, other bits become clear.
4. Drafting reveals the places where 'it' isn't right (yet) in ways that nothing else does.

Adapted from Delamont et al. (1997, p. 121).

Research diary

Many researchers keep a reflective research diary or logbook in which they record their ideas, discussions with fellow researchers, notions about the research process itself, and anything else pertinent to the whole of the research project and data analysis. This is a good idea for any researcher at any stage of their development. For some, the diary is a very personal document and reflects their own 'journey' through the research. For others it is a much broader document, more like what some have called a fieldwork journal or a research journal that includes a day-to-day commentary on the direction of the data collection and thoughts, ideas and inspirations about the analysis. You can use a diary format (large, page to a day book), loose-leaf journal, or – my preference – a large bound volume. Use this to record things like:

- what you did, and where, how and why you did it, with dates, possibly with an indication of time spent (so you can improve your time management);
- what you read (as a record that will contribute to your literature review as well as your analysis);
- contact summaries about what people, events or situations were involved, what the main themes or issues in the contact were, new hunches it generated and what new questions your next contact might address;
- what data you collected, how you processed them and what the outcomes were;
- particular achievements, dead ends and surprises (for example, when a puzzling episode suddenly becomes clear to you, or when you can finally see how a particular theory helps explain the situation you are analyzing);
- what you think or feel about what is happening – both in the field and in your analysis (for instance, whether you feel your analysis is procrustean or forced or if you feel there is some aspect of the setting you are investigating that you have not got a proper understanding of);
- any thoughts that come into your mind that may be relevant for your research (particularly new hunches that might arise from your reading of the literature or even from news items that help you see possible connections);
- anything else that influences you, especially thoughts about the future direction of your data collection and analysis.
  (Adapted from Miles and Huberman, 1994, pp. 50–4; Cryer, 2000, p. 99.)

Field notes

Field notes are contemporaneous notes taken while in the research setting (see Angrosino, 2007). They are partly mental notes (to help you remember who, what, why, when, where, etc.) and may be taken either whilst still in the field or immediately it is left in order to record key words, phrases and actions uttered and undertaken by the people you are investigating. Field notes are associated with and used especially in ethnography and participant observation, where they are a central technique for data collection. Writing up such notes by interpreting them, re-expressing them and using them both to create final reports and as examples in those reports is a core process in data analysis in ethnography. There are several important characteristics of field notes:

- They are not planned or structured. They are usually open-ended, loose, and often unruly and messy.
- They are a way of representing an event, of giving an account of it, not the event itself, and are therefore interpretations of the world. To write field notes you have to be selective. You have to identify certain things as significant – for your work or for those involved in the setting.
- They are descriptions of what people said and did, but they are not simply a recording of the facts. The accounts do not simply 'mirror' reality. As Emerson et al. put it, 'descriptive writing embodies and reflects particular purposes and commitments, and it also involves active processes of interpretation and sense-making' (Emerson et al., 2001, p. 353).
- Eventually, especially when written up, they accumulate into a corpus, a collection of writing that will form the basis for your qualitative analysis and provide examples for your reports.

Although field notes are usually associated with ethnography, jotted notes may also be collected by researchers using other approaches such as focus groups and interviews. Such researchers often write notes about their experience of data collection. For instance, those doing interviews may take notes about the conditions of the session (who was there as well as the interviewer and respondent, where it took place, whether the respondent was relaxed or for some reason was hurried or distracted) as well as noting any interruptions (children bursting in, fire alarm going off, phone calls, etc.). Some researchers do not fully trust their tape recorders and take notes about what was said and any other salient information (gestures, body language, expressions, demeanour). A common experience of researchers tape recording interviews is that respondents offer a lot more information, sometimes confidential and revealing, after the recorder has been switched off. To try and record this, researchers have to remember what was said and write it down at the first opportunity (sitting in their car after they have left the respondent, back at the bus station, etc.).

Writing up field notes

You need to write up these notes, as soon as you can, before the words and events fade from your memory. This process of writing up is actually the first step in your qualitative analysis. As you write up, you need to distinguish:

- Recording what happened, that is, describing things that went on.
- Recording your own actions, questions and reflections on what went on.

There is some debate about whether you should keep these kinds of notes separate or not. Some researchers like to keep separate what is primary data and what is commentary, reflection, analytic ideas and so on. For example, the developers of grounded theory (see Chapter 4) suggest there should be a strict separation between primary data, such as interviews, and commentary and analysis that is kept in memos, discussed later (Glaser and Strauss, 1967). Others, recognizing that even the primary data of field notes are not value-free and incorporate biases, perspectives and theories that reflect the analyst's view of the world, are less worried about keeping them distinct. How strict you are about this will depend on your own position on these issues. Nevertheless it is useful to remember the distinction and to recognize that there are degrees to which description is the product of interpretation.

The latter view is usually associated with a constructivist philosophy of research, but it also reflects an approach that is common amongst ethnographers who recognize that they cannot unthinkingly claim objectivity in their writings. This means not only that researchers must be careful about adopting an authoritative authorial voice without justification, but that their writing can, and perhaps should, include subjective factors like their own experiences and feelings and the emotions of those being studied. Van Maanen (1988) has distinguished three basic forms of presenting research findings in ethnography. These are summarized in Box 3.1. Although these illustrate a greater variety of possible approaches, in most areas of the social sciences, realist tales are still by far the most pervasive. However, as van Maanen admits, often what are, in the main, realist tales include sections that are confessional or impressionist.

Box 3.1 Van Maanen's Tales from the Field

Realist tales

Observations are reported as facts or documented by quotations from respondents or texts. Typical or common forms of the object of study are presented such as concrete details of daily life and routines. The views and beliefs of those being studied are emphasized. Sometimes the report may try to take a position of 'interpretive omnipotence' (Van Maanen, 1988, p. 51). The author, who is almost completely absent from the text, goes beyond subjective viewpoints to present wider, more general and more theoretical interpretations in a no-nonsense manner that is devoid of self-reflection and doubt.

(Continued)

(Continued)

Confessional tales

A more personalized account. The authors' views are made clear and the role they played in the research and in the interpretations is discussed. Authors' viewpoints are treated as an issue, as are methodological issues, such as the problems encountered in getting 'into the field' and in gathering data. The writing clearly separates personal and methodological confessions. Naturalness in presentation along with an account grounded in the data collected are used to show how what happened was a meeting between two cultures.

Impressionist tales

These take the form of a dramatic recounting of events often organized around striking stories and in chronological order. There is an attempt to create, by the inclusion of all the details associated with remembering, the sense of hearing, seeing and experiencing what the researcher did. Like a novel, the writer tries to make the audience feel they are in the field. Narratives are often used along with the conventions of textual identity, fragmented knowledge characterization and dramatic control.

Adapted from van Maanen (1988).

Strategies for writing field notes

Here are some common strategies for writing field notes. Use as many as you see fit.

- *Writer's prose.* Remember that the notes are not public documents so they can be biased and unguarded. No one else will see them; they are for your eyes only. In particular your informants won't see them so you can be candid.
- *Inscription and transcription.* Include descriptions of events and activities (inscriptions) and records of informants' own words and dialogues (transcriptions).
- *Recalling and ordering.* Put things in chronological order. Use key turning points, significant events, and be systematic in terms of topics of interest. You can write your notes with a post-hoc logic (what you learned later on informs them) or with dramatic representation (putting down only what you knew at the time, so that there are surprises as the story unfolds).
- *Rhetorical representations of action and dialogue.* Write sketches giving a snapshot of things using detailed imagery. Or write more of a story, with actions moving through time, sometimes building to a climax. This might even be developed into a field note tale, with fully realized characters, although unlike a novel this will not have a strong dramatic logic but rather, like real

life, will unfold aimlessly. You might even include dialogues, insofar as you can recall them.

- *Stance.* You need to decide on your distance from your respondents. Do you take an involved and sympathetic stance or do you remain neutral and disinterested?
- *Point of view.* Decide if the notes will be in the first person (I did this, I saw that) or third person (she did that, they did that together, he said this) or a mixture.
- *Emotions.* You may include accounts of your own emotions and feelings about the events or about the research in general. These can be useful because they mirror those of the informants, give analytical leads later, and can be used to identify biases and prejudices.

If all of this seems a lot to think about then remember, you are the expert. You were there. As Denzin notes:

> What is given in the text, what is written, is made up and fashioned out of memory and field notes. Writing of this order, writing that powerfully reinscribes and re-creates experience, invests itself with its own power and authority. No one else but this writer could have brought this new corner of the world alive in this way for the reader. (Denzin, 2004, p. 454)

Memos

Writers about grounded theory have popularized the use of memos as a way of performing qualitative analysis. Memos are seen as a way of theorizing and commenting as you go about thematic coding ideas and about the general development of the analytic framework. They are essentially notes to yourself (or to others in the research team) about the dataset. Glaser, one of the originators of grounded theory defined memos as

> ... the theorizing write-up of ideas about codes and their relationships as they strike the analyst while coding ... it can be a sentence, a paragraph or a few pages ... it exhausts the analyst's momentary ideation based on data with perhaps a little conceptual elaboration. (Glaser, 1978, pp. 83–4)

As I mentioned above, grounded theorists tend to suggest keeping the kind of analytic ideas that appear in memos strictly separate from the primary documents (interview transcripts, field notes, collected documents, etc.). This is partly because of the need to remain grounded in the data, and you therefore need to know what are data and what is your commentary. Moreover, as originally conceived, memos are about the coding of the data. Coding is discussed in more detail in the next chapter, but essentially it is the process of identifying passages (in the field notes or interviews) that exemplify certain thematic ideas and giving them a label – the code. Memos are analytic thoughts about the codes and they provide clarification and direction during coding. However, they also form the next step in analysis from coding to reporting. Memos often include ideas and extended discussions that can be included in your final reports.

Other analysts are more flexible in the way they use memos. One idea suggested by Richardson, following Glaser and Strauss (1967), is to organize your notes into four categories (this can also be used if you integrate these into field notes or write these ideas in your research diary). Mark each clearly on the page using the letters in brackets. They are:

- *Observation notes (ON)*. As concrete and detailed as possible about what you saw, heard, felt, tasted, etc.
- *Methodological notes (MN)*. Notes to yourself about how to collect 'data' – who to talk to, what to wear, when to phone, and so on.
- *Theoretical notes (TN)*. Hunches, hypotheses, connections, alternative interpretations, critiques of what you are doing/thinking/seeing.
- *Personal notes (PN)*. These are your feelings about the research, who you are talking to, your doubts, anxieties and pleasures.
  (Adapted from Richardson, 2004, p. 489.)

Memos should be written throughout the research, from when you start data collection until you complete your report. Always give priority to writing memos, as the inspiration strikes you. Once the flow starts, keep at it. It doesn't matter how long the memos are. They can be modified and split up later if need be. Like field notes, memos are for your eyes only. So you can be forthright and they do not have to be polished pieces of writing. Try to keep memos at a conceptual level and avoid talking about the features of individuals except as examples of the general concepts. You might not follow this strictly if you are doing a case analysis, but still try to keep your comments about cases at a conceptual level. Box 3.2 summarizes what memos can be written about.

Box 3.2 The uses of memos

1. *A new idea for a code.* This may be sparked off by something a respondent says. Keep a list of codes handy to help cross-referencing.

(Continued)

(Continued)

2. *Just a quick hunch.* Indicate what's just a hunch or conjecture and what is supported by evidence in the data. Otherwise you'll come back later and think that a mere hunch is actually supported by the evidence. (It may or may not be.)

3. *Integrative discussion* (e.g. of previous reflective remarks). Often this brings together one or more memos and/or code definitions. A key activity here is to compare codes, settings or cases.

4. *As a dialogue amongst researchers.* Memos are a good way of sharing analytic ideas with co-workers. Put your name and date on the memo so you know who wrote it and when.

5. *To question the quality of the data.* You may feel that the respondent was not entirely open about something or that they are not qualified to tell you about an issue, i.e. the story is second or third hand.

6. *To question the original analytic framework.* You might write a memo against an existing code to raise questions about whether it actually makes sense. Consider combining codes if memos on them look similar. This is often an indication that the codes are actually about the same thing.

7. *What is puzzling or surprising about a case?* A key skill in examining qualitative documents is to be able to spot what is surprising. Sometimes we are too familiar with the context to find something surprising or more commonly we simply fail to spot it.

8. *As alternative hypotheses to another memo.* This is a kind of internal dialogue between those involved on the project or to yourself if you are working alone.

9. *If you have no clear idea but are struggling to find one.* You may think you are onto something, in that case writing it down may help sort out what the issues are. Remember you can always come back to what you have written later to see if, in the cold light of the next day, it still makes sense.

10. *To raise a general theme or metaphor.* This is a more integrative or holistic activity. At some time in your analysis you will need to start trying to bring the manifold issues together.

Adapted from Gibbs (2002, pp. 88–9),

Writing up the report

If you have been writing throughout your project, keeping a journal and writing memos, then the task of writing a final report will be much less daunting. You will already have many passages and perhaps whole chapters that can form part of it. Even so, the task can seem intimidating. However, there is no need to start at Chapter 1, just start with the easiest chapter or section. That will make it less difficult to begin and to make progress, and the more writing you have done, the better you will feel about the project and the more confidence and clarity you will have about the rest of your write-up.

Some writers start with a list or outline of what they want to say and then work through it developing their ideas. Others find it best to start with a statement of purpose or objective for their work and then write on from there. When writing, some people like to produce one sentence at a time, polishing each one before moving on to the next. In contrast, others prefer to free-write. They get it all down as fast as they can and then go back and tidy it up. One professor I know likes to work on several pieces at once. He will spend an hour on one then move to another and spend an hour or two on that. That's not for me; I find it hard enough to focus just on the one piece I am writing. Choose whichever approach suits you, even whatever suits you at the time, as long as you don't give up writing.

Organizing the report

You need to find an organizing structure that can bring together all your disparate ideas into a coherent 'story'. Such a structure will often appear as chapters or sections in your report. For example, in the simplest case you might give a chronological account where each section is an episode from your study, or a case-by-case account, where each section discusses one case. Table 3.2 gives some other alternatives.

TABLE 3.2   Organizing the qualitative report

1. A set of individual case studies, followed by a discussion of differences and similarities between cases.
2. An account structured around the main themes identified, drawing illustrative examples from each transcript (or other text) as required.
3. A thematic presentation of the findings, using a different individual case study to illustrate each of the main themes.

Adapted from King (1998).

Focus

Another key to the organization of a report is its focus. To start with, this will be unclear, but as you progress through your analysis and your writing it should gradually emerge. You will know you have a focus when you can complete the sentence: 'the purpose of this study is …'. You may find that talking over your research with colleagues or friends helps you to recognize what the focus should be, because in order to explain it to them you will need to identify a central idea on which to hang your explanations.

Writers on grounded theory have made getting a focus a crucial part of their approach, though they disagree on the extent to which the focus of the analysis should be based on concepts that arise out of the concerns of the respondents themselves, or how far they should be informed by social science theory and concepts. The idea is that at some point in coding and analysis a core or central category will emerge as something around which narrative and conceptual description can be woven. Glaser, one of the founders of grounded theory, believes that the core category can be discovered and should be strongly grounded in the data collected. It is a central and recurrent conceptual entity, substantially and richly connected to other categories and with considerable analytic power. It accounts for much of the variation in a pattern of behaviour 'which is relevant and problematic for those involved' in the situation studied (Glaser, 1978, p. 93). Those of a more constructivist bent, such as Charmaz (1990), prefer to see the analysis as something that emerges. For Charmaz the core category is something that the researcher brings to the data. It is the result of a process of interpretation, not simply something there to be discovered. This makes it harder to identify and it may take some time and considerable development of the coding before a candidate for the central category becomes clear.

Whatever view you take, the important point is that this central idea or category has explanatory power. Many, if not most, of the other thematic ideas you have identified can be related to it or explained by it. Thus much of the variation in relevant behaviour, actions, language and experiences can be explained by reference to it, and it should even be capable of explaining contradictory or alternative cases (though you may need to refer to additional factors along with it).

Redrafting

Becker points out that one of the bad habits in writing that a lot of undergraduates get into is thinking that the first draft is the final draft. In his book on writing in the social sciences (Becker, 1986) he demonstrates how much redrafting, editing and tightening is necessary in order to write a decent final report. The aim of redrafting is to re-express your writing to make it clearer, read better and flow more easily. One of the most important aspects of this is to cut out redundant material. Look for needless repetition and delete it. Box 3.3 lists some guidelines to use when redrafting.

Box 3.3   Guidelines for revising the first draft

1. Read the text through and ask yourself:

   - what am I trying to say?
   - who is the text for?
   - what changes will make the text clearer and easier to follow?

   (Continued)

(Continued)

2. Global or big changes (e.g. rewriting sections) you might consider are:

   - reordering parts of the text;
   - rewriting sections;
   - adding examples or removing duplicate examples;
   - changing the examples for better ones;
   - deleting parts that seem confusing.

3. Minor text changes you might consider are:

   - simpler wording;
   - shorter sentences;
   - shorter paragraphs;
   - active rather than passive tenses;
   - substituting positive constructions for negatives;
   - writing sequences in order;
   - spacing numbered sequences or lists down the page (as here).

4. Read the revised text through to see if you want to make any further global changes.
5. Finally, repeat this whole procedure some time (say 24 hours) after making your original revisions, and do it without looking back at the original text.

Adapted from Hartley (1989, p. 90).

All writers, no matter how experienced, can gain from getting feedback from others. It is very hard to distance yourself from your own words. You know them too well. So get friends or colleagues, preferably those who have at least a little knowledge about your topic, to read your drafts. It is helpful if you tell them what kind of feedback you want. Is the draft too long, so you want to know what can be cut? Is the style appropriate for the intended audience? Do you need the contents checked for accuracy and detail (rather than style)? If you tell your readers what feedback you want, they won't waste their time picking up all the small spelling mistakes when all you need is to know what parts you could cut. Don't seek feedback from readers before you have a proper first draft, but at the same time the draft they see does not have to be well polished. As long as you can revise and improve the text there is no problem. As Becker notes, 'the only version that counts is the last one' (Becker, 1986, p. 21).

Style

Traditionally, the style in which reports, papers, theses and so on have been written has been a rather dry, technical one. Writers presented the basic story using the passive voice and the past tense. Respondents' own words were used, but only to a limited degree and usually only in illustrative quotations. This reflected the predominant scientific and realist stance taken by social scientists. Research could reveal the true underlying nature of social reality and the write-up could represent that reality in a simple, straightforward and objective manner.

However, in recent years, starting in anthropology and spreading rapidly to other disciplines, there has been a realization that there could be problems with this view. These have centred on issues like authority, objectivity and reflexivity. Authority is the implicit claim that the researcher can give an account of how things really are that goes beyond that given by the people involved, in fact that might not even be understood or accepted by those people. An allied quality of the analysis is its claimed objectivity, its freedom from bias or partiality. Reflexivity is the awareness and acknowledgement of the role of the researcher in the construction of knowledge. Underlying these problems was the recognition that all qualitative research involves interpretation and that researchers needed to be reflective about the implications of their methods, values, biases and decisions for the knowledge of the social world they create (see Chapter 7).

This has had widespread implications for the way social science research is carried out and, in particular, how it is written. One consequence has been a widening of the standards expected of social science writing and in some cases an experimentation with radically different forms of reporting such as dialogues and debates. It has engendered a growing awareness of the range of styles in which qualitative analysis can be reported. One example of this is the three forms of presentation of ethnography findings suggested by van Maanen and summarized in Box 3.1.

You may wish to experiment with how you present your results, but beware; readers generally expect texts to follow a genre or style. Examples include the community studies report, the anthropological monograph, the evaluation report, the scientific paper, the popular magazine article, and so on. A common format in academic journals as well as undergraduate dissertations and PhD theses is: Introduction – Literature review – Research design/methods – Results/Analysis – Discussion – Conclusion.

In qualitative research the presentation of the results and the discussion of them are frequently rather more interwoven, but this overall structure is very widespread. It is important when writing up your analysis that you make yourself aware of the traditions and styles of writing in your field and make clear how your text relates to the others – even if you have chosen to reject the dominant forms. You therefore need to know and be aware of the audience you intend to address. They will have a set of expectations about what they will read and how it will be written. Key amongst these readers are the reviewers of journal articles and the examiners of dissertations and theses. Ignore their expectations at your own peril.

Key points

- It is important that you do not leave all your writing until late in the analysis, not least because writing is an essential part of thinking about your data. It helps you clarify your thinking and can be shared with others to get feedback. Keeping all your hunches, ideas, notes, reflections, actions and so on in a research diary is a good idea.
- Field notes are records of what happened when you were 'in the field'. However, they are never simple descriptions, they are inevitably interpretations and often include the researcher's experiences, feelings, biases and impressions.
- Memos are notes to yourself about your developing analysis. Like field notes they can contain observations, methodological and theoretical ideas, as well as more personal reflections. Memos are a way of recording and sharing your emerging analytic ideas.
- At some stage you need to produce reports about your research. This can include many of the ideas and examples you have recorded in your diary, field notes and memos, but it needs a focus. It needs a core idea or theme, which is central in explaining the many events, situations, actions and other phenomena that your report discusses.

Further reading

Debates and suggestions about writing notes and reports are found in more detail in the following works:

Angrosino, M. (2007) *Doing Ethnographic and Observational Research*. (Book 3 of *The SAGE Qualitative Research Kit*), London: Sage.
Becker, H.S. (1986) *Writing for Social Scientists: How to Start and Finish Your Thesis, Book or Article*. Chicago: University of Chicago Press.
Emerson, R.M., Fretz, R.I. and Shaw, L.L. (1995) *Writing Ethnographic Fieldnotes*. Chicago: University of Chicago Press.
Wolcott, H.F. (2001) *Writing Up Qualitative Research* (2nd ed.). Newbury Park, CA: Sage.

4
Thematic coding and categorizing

Chapter objectives
After reading this chapter, you should

- see the central role of coding in qualitative analysis;
- see from the close examination of an example the importance of creating codes that are analytic and theoretical and not merely descriptive; and
- know two techniques that can be used to promote the move from description to analysis: constant comparison and line-by-line coding.

Codes and coding

Coding is how you define what the data you are analyzing are about. It involves identifying and recording one or more passages of text or other data items such as the parts of pictures that, in some sense, exemplify the same theoretical or descriptive idea. Usually, several passages are identified and they are then linked with a name for that idea – the code. Thus all the text and so on that is about the same thing or exemplifies the same thing is coded to the same name. Coding is a way of indexing or categorizing the text in order to establish a framework of thematic ideas about it (see Box 4.1 for a discussion of these terms). Coding in this way enables two forms of analysis.

1. You can retrieve all the text coded with the same label to combine passages that are all examples of the same phenomenon, idea, explanation or activity. This form of retrieval is a very useful way of managing or organizing the data, and enables the researcher to examine the data in a structured way.
2. You can use the list of codes, especially when developed into a hierarchy, to examine further kinds of analytic questions, such as relationships between the codes (and the text they code) and case-by-case comparisons. This will be examined in Chapter 6.

Box 4.1   Code, index, category or theme?

When you first come across it, the idea of a code might seem rather mysterious. You probably first think about it in terms of secret codes and ciphers. For others, the association with computer code and programming might come to mind. As it is used here, codes are neither secretive nor to do with programming. They are simply a way of organizing your thinking about the text and your research notes.

Writers on qualitative analysis use a variety of terms to talk about codes and coding. Terms such as indices, themes and categories are used. Each reflects an important aspect of coding. Richie and Lewis prefer the term 'index' as this captures the sense in which codes refer to one or more passages in the text about the same topic in the way that entries in a book index refer to passages in the book (Ritchie et al., 2003). In phenomenological analysis, a term that is used instead of codes is 'themes' (Smith, 1995 ; King, 1998). Again this captures something of the spirit of what is involved in linking sections of text with thematic ideas that reveal the person's experience of the world. Dey (1993) uses 'category', which indicates another aspect of coding. The application of names to passages of text is not arbitrary, it involves a deliberate and thoughtful process of categorizing the content of the text. Coding means recognizing that not only are there different examples of things in the text but that there are different *types* of things referred to.

To add confusion to this, quantitative researchers also use the term 'coding' when assigning numbers to survey question answers or categorizing answers to open-ended questions. The latter is somewhat like qualitative coding, but is usually done in order to count the categorized responses, which is not the prime motivation of qualitative researchers.

The structured list of codes and the rules for their application (their definitions) that result from qualitative analysis are sometimes referred to as a coding frame. Again, this is confusing, since quantitative researchers use this to refer to the listing that tells them what numeric value to assign to different answers in surveys so that they can be counted. For that reason I have avoided the term. Others use the term 'thematic framework' (Ritchie et al., 2003) or 'template' (King,

(Continued)

(Continued)

1998). Here I just refer to the list of codes, or the codebook, a term used by many other analysts. 'Book' suggests something more weighty than just a list and indeed it is good practice that you should keep more than just a list. The codebook is something that should be kept separate from any coded transcripts. It should include not only the current and complete list of your codes, arranged hierarchically if appropriate, but also a definition for each along with any memos or analytic notes about the coding scheme that you have written.

Coding is easiest using a transcript. It is possible to code directly from an audio or video recording or from rough field notes, but it is neither easy to do this nor is it easy to retrieve the sections of recording or notes that have been coded when you need them. (The exception to this is when you are using CAQDAS and digital video or audio. Then the software makes it much easier to retrieve the sections of video or audio that you have coded.) In fact, a lot of the time, coding is best done with an electronic text file using dedicated analysis software. I shall examine this in Chapter 9, but here I shall explain techniques that can be done with a paper transcript. I actually use both paper-based and computer-based approaches myself. I find that paper allows me the kinds of creativity, flexibility and ease of access that is important at the early stages of analysis. I then transfer the coding ideas into the electronic version of the project in order to continue the analysis. Do not be afraid about using either just paper or just software or both. As long as you make certain preparations (like introducing your data into the software before you produce printed copy to work on), there is nothing to stop you moving, when you want to, from paper to the software. Of course, you don't have to use software at all. For most of the last century, those undertaking qualitative analysis did not or could not use software. Most of the classic studies using qualitative research were undertaken without electronic assistance.

Code definitions

Codes form a focus for thinking about the text and its interpretation. The actual coded text is just one aspect of that. For this reason it is important that as early as you can you write some notes about each code you develop. In the previous chapter I introduced the idea of writing memos as an important way of recording the development of your analytic thinking. A key function of such memos is to note the nature of a code and the thinking that lies behind it and to explain how the code should be applied or what kinds of text, images, and so on should be linked to the code. Keeping such a record is important for two reasons:

1. It will help you apply the code in a consistent way. Without having to reread all the text already coded to this name, you will be able to decide if any new text should really be coded there.

2. If you are working in a team, it will enable you to share your codes with others for them to use and, if they have done the same, to use theirs. It is quite likely, if more than one member of the team is coding, that more than one person will come up with similar coding ideas. Having memos about the codes will enable you to tell if the codes are, in fact, identical or not.

Keep your code memos in one or more word-processing files (so you can easily edit them or print them out) or use large filing cards to record the details. Typically you will need to record:

- The label or name of the code that you have used in marking up and coding the transcript.
- Who coded it – the name of the researcher (not needed if you are working alone).
- The date when the coding was done or changed.
- Definition of the code – a description of the analytic idea it refers to and ways of ensuring that the coding is reliable, that is, carried out in a systematic and consistent way.
- Any other notes of your thinking about the code, for example, ideas you may have about how it relates to other codes or a hunch that maybe the text coded here could actually be split between two different codes (see Box 3.2 for more ideas).

The mechanics of coding

Those new to coding often find one of the most challenging things to begin with is identifying chunks of text and working out what codes they represent in a way that is theoretical and analytic and not merely descriptive. This involves careful reading of the text and deciding what it is about. In the visual arts the term 'intensive seeing' is used to refer to the way that we can pay close attention to all the things we can see, even the commonplace and ordinary. In the same way, you need to undertake 'intensive reading' when coding. Charmaz suggests some basic questions to ask as you undertake this intensive reading that will help you get started:

- What is going on?
- What are people doing?
- What is the person saying?

41

- What do these actions and statements take for granted?
- How do structure and context serve to support, maintain, impede or change these actions and statements? (Charmaz, 2003, pp. 94–5)

An example

To illustrate this initial stage, consider the following example. It is taken from a study of carers for people with dementia and is an interview with Barry, who is now looking after his wife, who has Alzheimer's disease. The interviewer has just asked Barry, 'Have you had to give anything up that you enjoyed doing that was important to you?', and he replies:

```
1    BARRY
2    Well, the only thing that we've really given up is – well we used to
3    go dancing. Well she can't do it now so I have to go on my own,
4    that's the only thing really. And then we used to go indoor bowling
5    at the sports centre. But of course, that's gone by the board now. So
6    we don't go there. But I manage to get her down to works club, just
7    down the road on the occasional Saturdays, to the dances. She'll sit
8    and listen to the music, like, stay a couple of hours and then she's
9    had enough. And then, if it's a nice weekend I take her out in the
10   car.
```

Description

At one level this is a very simple reply. In lines 2 to 6 Barry gives two examples of things that he and Beryl used to enjoy together, dancing and indoor bowling, then, without prompting, he lists two things that they still do together, visiting dances at the works club and going out for a drive. So a first idea is to code lines 2 to 4 to the code 'Dancing', lines 4 to 6 to 'Indoor bowling', 6 to 9 to 'Dances at works club' and 9 to 10 to 'Drive together'. Such coding might be useful if you are analyzing interviews with lots of carers and you wanted to examine the actual activities given up and those still done together and compare them between couples. Then retrieving all the text coded at codes about such activities would enable you to list and compare what people said about them.

Categorization

However, such coding is simply descriptive; there are usually better ways to categorize the things mentioned and there are other things indicated by Barry's text. In analysis you need to move away from descriptions, especially using respondent's terms, to a more categorical, analytic and theoretical level of coding. For example, you can code the text about dancing and indoor bowling together at a code 'Joint activities ceased', and text on works club dances and driving together to the code 'Joint activities continuing'. Assuming you have done the same in other interviews, you can now retrieve all the text about what couples have given up doing and see if they have things in common. In so doing you have begun to categorize the text.

Analytic codes

Thinking about this suggests another way to code the text. Both dancing and bowling are physical activities involving some degree of skilled movement. Clearly Beryl has lost that, so we could code lines 2 to 6 to the code 'Loss of physical co-ordination'. This code is now slightly more analytic than those we started with, which just repeated Barry's descriptions. Barry does not talk about loss of physical co-ordination, but it is implied in what he says. Of course you need to be careful. This is an interpretation, based, here, on very little evidence. You need to look for other examples in Barry's interview of the same thing and perhaps other evidence in what he says of Beryl's infirmity.

Another thing to notice about this text is the way Barry changes from using 'we' about what they used to do together, to saying 'I' when he turns to the things they do now. This suggests another pair of analytic codes, one about joint activity with a sense of being a couple, the other about activity where the carer is just doing things for his partner. You might code these as 'Togetherness' and 'Doing for'. Note that these codes do not simply code what happened, but rather suggest the way in which Barry thought about, or conceptualized, these things.

Other things you might have noticed about the passage that might be candidates for codes include Barry's rhetorical use of 'Well' in lines 2 and 3. He says it three times. Is this an indication of a sense of resignation, loss or regret? Again, from such a short passage it is not clear. But you might code it 'Resignation' for now and later see if it is consistent with other text of Barry's you have coded to 'Resignation'. It is interesting to note that Barry says he still goes dancing, on his own. A different interpretation of this use of 'well' and the fact that it is the first thing that Barry mentions, is that dancing was a key thing that he and Beryl did together as a couple. You might therefore think that it is a kind of core or central activity of the couple, something that was central to their life together as a couple. Again, it would be useful to examine other carers to see if there are similar defining activities and to see if this identifies any differences between carers. Perhaps carers where the defining activities have been less affected by Alzheimer's are different from those where it has.

In summary, here are the codes that might be used to code the passage by Barry.

- *Descriptive codes*: 'Dancing', 'Indoor bowling', 'Dances at works club', 'Drive together'.
- *Categories*: 'Joint activities ceased', 'Joint activities continuing'.
- *Analytic codes*: 'Loss of physical co-ordination', 'Togetherness', 'Doing for', 'Resignation', 'Core activity'.

Of course, it is unlikely that you would use all these codes to code just one short passage like this, but I have used them here to illustrate the way you need to move from descriptive coding, close to the respondent's terms, to categorization and to more analytic and theoretical codes. Also notice that I have used the codes only once in this short text. Normally, you would look through the rest of the text to see if there are any more passages that can be coded to the same code and do the same with other participants.

How you develop these thematic codes and which of them you focus on will depend on the aim of the research. In many cases, research is driven by funding bodies and what you have agreed with the funders that you will do. For example, if the research on those suffering from Alzheimer's disease was funded by the bodies that provide services to carers, then you might focus on the themes 'Doing for' and 'Joint activities'. On the other hand, if you were doing a PhD on the social psychology of couples, you might focus on 'Core activity' and 'Togetherness'.

Marking the coding

When using paper, coding is done by jotting the code name in the margin or by marking text with colour (either in the margin or using highlighter pens). Figure 4.1 shows some of these ways of indicating this coding on the transcript. There are boxes with linked names (I used arrows), shading (e.g. with a highlighter pen) and linked code name. The right-hand margin is used with brackets to indicate the lines coded. I have circled or highlighted some key words or terms such as emotive words, unusual terms, metaphors and words used for emphasis.

Data-driven or concept-driven?

The construction of codes in a codebook is an analytic process. It is the building up of a conceptual schema. Although in the illustrations I have discussed the codes were derived from and are grounded in the data, it is possible to build a codebook without initial reference to the data collected.

Concept-driven coding

The categories or concepts the codes represent may come from the research literature, previous studies, topics in the interview schedule, hunches you have about what is going on, and so on. It is possible to construct a collection of codes in a

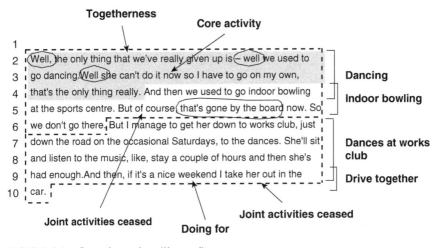

FIGURE 4.1   Barry's reply with coding

codebook without, at first, using them to code the data. Such a view is taken by Ritchie et al.(2003) in their advocacy of framework analysis. In framework analysis, before applying codes to the text, the researcher is encouraged to build up a list of key thematic ideas. These can be taken from the literature and previous research but are also generated by reading through at least some of the transcripts and other documents such as field notes, focus groups and printed documents. A similar view is taken by King (1998), who recommends the construction of a template, using similar sources of inspiration, which is a hierarchical arrangement of potential codes. In both King's template analysis and framework analysis, coding consists of the identification of chunks of text that exemplify the codes in this initial list. However, all these authors recognize that the researcher will need to amend the list of codes during analysis as new ideas and new ways of categorizing are detected in the text.

Data-driven coding

The opposite of starting with a given list of codes is to start with none. This approach is usually called open coding (see the discussion later in this chapter), perhaps because one tries to do it with an open mind. Of course, no one starts with absolutely no ideas. The researcher is both an observer of the social world and a part of that same world. We all have ideas of what we might expect to be happening and as social scientists we are likely to have more than most as a result of our awareness of theoretical ideas and empirical research. Nevertheless one can try, as far as possible, not to start with preconceptions. Simply start by reading the texts and trying to tease out what is happening. Such an approach is taken by the advocates of grounded theory (Glaser and Strauss, 1967; Strauss, 1987; Glaser,

45

1992; Strauss and Corbin, 1997; Charmaz, 2003) and by many phenomenologists in their concept of bracketing – setting aside presuppositions, prejudices and preliminary ideas about phenomena (Moustakas, 1994; Maso, 2001; Giorgi and Giorgi, 2003). But even they accept that a complete *tabula rasa* approach is unrealistic. The point is that, as far as possible, one should try to pull out from the data what is happening and not impose an interpretation based on pre-existing theory.

These two approaches to generating codes are not exclusive. Most researchers move backwards and forwards between both sources of inspiration during their analysis. The possibility of constructing codes before or separately from an examination of the data will reflect, to some extent, the inclination, knowledge and theoretical sophistication of the researcher. If your project has been defined in the context of a clear theoretical framework, then it is likely that you will have some good ideas about what potential codes you will need. That is not to say that they will be preserved intact throughout the project, but at least it gives you a starting point for the kinds of phenomena you want to look for when reading the text. The trick here is not to become too tied to the initial codes you construct.

What to code

The example of coding I have discussed above is very short and specific to one context – caring for those suffering from dementia. What about interviews, notes and recordings on other topics? What other kind of things can be coded? The answer depends to some extent on the kind of analysis you are intending to do. Some disciplines and theoretical approaches like phenomenology, discourse analysis or conversation analysis will require that you pay special attention to certain kinds of phenomena in the texts you are examining.

Fortunately, for a very wide range of types of qualitative analysis that includes much policy and applied research and evaluation work as well as interpretive and hermeneutic approaches, there is a common ground of phenomena that researchers tend to look for in their texts. Some typical examples are listed in Table 4.1. Different authors have a different emphasis, but many of the ideas in the table will be useful to any analysis of texts.

Note that many of the examples in this table are rather descriptive. I have given these because it is easier to illustrate the phenomena with concrete examples. However, as I have suggested above, it is necessary to move from descriptions, especially those couched simply in terms used by participants, to more general and analytic categories. For example, rather than the event 'Joining a sports club' you might want to code this text to 'Activity to make friends' or 'Commitment to keeping fit' or even 'Identity as a fit person', which make reference to the more general significance of this event.

TABLE 4.1   What can be coded? (with examples)

1. Specific acts, behaviours – what people do or say.

    Avoiding the question. Getting the opinions of friends.

2. Events – these are usually brief, one-off events or things someone has done. It is not uncommon for the respondent to tell them as a story.

    Being rejected at job interview. Moving into a homeless hostel. Finding husband has another woman. Joining a sports club.

3. Activities – these are of longer duration than acts and often take place in a particular setting and may have several people involved.

    Going dancing. Taking a training course. Helping partner with dementia get washed and dressed. Working in a bar.

4. Strategies, practices or tactics – activities aimed towards some goal.

    Using word of mouth to find jobs. Getting divorced for financial reasons. Entering a relationship to get somewhere to live.

5. States – general conditions experienced by people or found in organizations.

    Resignation, e.g. 'At my age it's hard to find work.' Working extra hours to get the job done.

6. Meanings – a wide range of phenomena at the core of much qualitative analysis. Meanings and interpretations are important parts of what directs participants' actions.

    (a) What concepts do participants use to understand their world? What norms, values, rules and mores guide their actions?

    The idea of 'on-sight climbing' amongst rock climbers to describe doing a climb without inspection, artificial aids, pre-placed protection or pre-vious practice, with the implication that this is a superior way of doing a climb.

    (b) What meaning or significance does it have for participants, how do they construe events, what are their feelings?

    Blame, e.g. 'His letter made me feel I was to blame.'

    (c) What symbols do people use to understand their situation? What names do they use for objects, events, persons, roles, settings and equipment?

    Delivery van referred to as 'the old bus' (affectionately or dismissively). Teaching referred to as 'work at the chalkface' (like work at the coalface, not administration).

7. Participation – people's involvement or adaptation to a setting.

    Adjusting to a new job, e.g. 'I find I have to be careful what I say now, because I know about things before they are finalized.'

(Continued)

TABLE 4.1 (*Continued*)

8. Relationships or interaction – between people, considered simultaneously.

    Enjoying the family, e.g. ' . . . they're 26 and 21 and most boys of that age are married, but mine aren't and they like to come home, have friends to stay. I like that.'

9. Conditions or constraints – the precursor to or cause of events or actions, things that restrict behaviour or actions.

    Firm's loss of markets (before lay-offs). Divorce (before financial difficulties).

10. Consequences – What happens if . . .

    Experience gets jobs, e.g. 'So what you get is, people that haven't got no qualification, but have got a few months' experience are walking into jobs.'

11. Settings – the entire context of the events under study.

    Hostel for the homeless. Training college. Day care centre.

12. Reflexive – the researcher's role in the process, how intervention generated the data.

    Expressing sympathy, e.g. 'It must be hard for you in that situation.'

Adapted from Strauss (1987), Bogdan and Biklen (1992), Mason (1996).

Retrieving text from codes

So far I have discussed coding mainly as a way of analyzing the content of the text. However, coding also has another, important purpose, which is to enable the methodical retrieval of thematically related sections of the text. There are several reasons for this:

- You can quickly collect together all the text coded in the same way and read it through to see what is at the core of the code.
- You can examine how, within a case, a coded thematic idea changes or is affected by other factors.
- You can explore how categorizations or thematic ideas represented by the codes vary from case to case, from setting to setting or from incident to incident.

Such retrieval activities will help you develop your analysis and your analytic and theoretical approach. For example, by reading the text you have coded to what might be a rather descriptive code used across several cases, you may discover some deeper, more analytic connection. You can then rename the code and rewrite its definition to indicate this idea, or perhaps create a new code and code relevant text to it.

Practical retrieval

In order to retrieve the text to do this, you need to have taken some practical measures with your coded transcripts. All these kinds of retrieval are easiest if you are using CAQDAS. I will explore how in Chapter 8. If you are using paper you will need to do two things:

1. Gather together all the text coded with the same code in one place. You should produce many photocopies of your coded transcript so that you can cut up the sheets and store extracts with the same code in separate paper wallets, envelopes or files. If using a word processor, this can be achieved by copying and pasting the text into separate files for each code.
2. Tag or label each extract (paper slip or electronically cut-and-pasted text) so that you can tell which document it came from. (If you use line numbers, these will tell you whereabouts in the document it came from. However, note that if you are cutting and pasting in a word processor, line numbering will not be preserved in the copy. In this case it is best simply to add a reference to the original line numbers along with the source tag.) If you have just a few documents, then just a couple of initials at the top of each extract to identify the document will do. But if you have a large number of documents/respondents, then a numbering system will help. A tag consisting of a string of letters or numbers that indicates not only the identity of the respondent but also some basic biographical information (like age group, gender and status) will help identify where the original text came from. You might use something like 'BBm68R' to indicate the interview with Barry Bentlow who is male, aged 68 and retired. Put this tag at the top of each extract or slip.

Such retrieval of the text coded by one code should be kept with any memos about the code so that you can ensure that the definition of the code still makes sense across all the extracts retrieved. If not you may need to recode some of the text or change the code definition. You can also check if any of your analytic ideas recorded in the memo elucidate the text you have retrieved or possibly write more in the memo after examining the retrieved text.

Grounded theory

One of the most commonly used approaches to coding is grounded theory. This approach has been used extensively across a variety of social science disciplines and it lies behind the design of much CAQDAS. Its central focus is on inductively generating novel theoretical ideas or hypotheses from the data as opposed to testing theories specified beforehand. Insofar as these new theories 'arise' out of the data and are supported by the data, they are said to be grounded. It is only at a later stage of the analysis that these new ideas need to be related to existing theory. In their very accessible account of grounded theory, Strauss and Corbin (1990) present many specific ideas and techniques for achieving a grounded analysis. They divide coding into three stages:

1. *Open coding*, where the text is read reflectively to identify relevant categories.
2. *Axial coding*, where categories are refined, developed and related or interconnected.
3. *Selective coding*, where the 'core category', or central category that ties all other categories in the theory together into a story, is identified and related to other categories.

Open coding

This is the kind of coding where you examine the text by making comparisons and asking questions. Strauss and Corbin also suggest it is important to avoid a label that is merely a description of the text. You need to try and formulate theoretical or analytic codes. The actual text is always an example of a more general phenomenon and the code title should indicate this more general idea. This is the hard part of coding. As you read the text, phrase by phrase, you should constantly ask questions: who, when, where, what, how, how much, why, and so on. This is designed to alert you to the theoretical issues lying behind the text and to give you a sensitivity to the deeper theoretical levels in them.

Constant comparison

There are also several contrasts one can construct to help understand what might lie behind the surface text. The idea behind these contrasts or comparisons is to try to bring out what is distinctive about the text and its content. All too often we are so familiar with things that we fail to notice what is significant. Think about comparisons all the time as you go through doing your coding. This is one aspect of what is referred to as the method of constant comparison (Glaser and Strauss, 1967). Here are some examples of techniques suggested by Strauss, and Corbin (1990).

Analysis of word, phrase or sentence   Pick out one word or phrase that seems significant, then list all its possible meanings. Examine the text to see which apply here. You may find new meanings that were not obvious beforehand.

Flip-flop technique   Compare extremes on a dimension in question. For example, if someone mentions their age is a problem in finding work, try to contrast this with what it would be like for someone very young, just entering the job market, and someone else near the end of their working life. You may discover dimensions or issues you hadn't thought of before, such as the interaction of age and skills. Older people may lack new skills, but young people lack general work experience skills.

Systematic comparison   Ask a series of 'what ifs' to explore all the dimensions of two phenomena. How do they differ, how do people respond differently? These are to try to stimulate you to recognize what is already there. For example, you can:

- Ask what if the circumstances, order of events, characteristics of the people, places, settings and so on were different.
- Ask how are the events and so on like and unlike others.
- Take a key element and free associate or read the text parts in a different order to try to stimulate ideas of what is in the text.

Far-out comparisons   Take one element of the concept you are examining and think of the most remote or different example of some other phenomenon that shares some characteristics with that concept. Then work through all the other elements of both phenomena to see if they shed any light on the original. For example, you might compare a homeless man with a man who has had an arm amputated. Both suffer loss. Those without limbs experience stigma. Is that the same for the homeless? Those experiencing stigma deal with it by avoiding public places (hiding away), passing it off as others' problem and so on. Do the homeless do the same? Alternatively, you might compare the homeless who talk about their bad luck with gamblers' talk of a run of bad luck. Gamblers overestimate the extent to which they can control events. Is that the same for those looking for a home? In these cases the point about the comparison is to generate more codes that form dimensions, properties or aspects of the original idea.

Waving the red flag   Be sensitive to phrases like 'Never', 'Always', 'It couldn't possibly be that way'. They are signals to look more closely. It is rarely the case that they are actually true. They usually mean things shouldn't happen that way. You need to find out what would happen if that situation actually did occur.

All these are good ways of encouraging more creative and deeper thinking about what is in the text. But in addition to these kinds of imaginative comparisons, it is important to carry out other kinds of comparisons. For example, you should compare what you have just coded with other text you have coded earlier or coded in a similar way. You can also compare the case you are working on with other cases you have researched. As you create new codes and code new text, it is worth checking to see whether text previously coded this way still makes sense now you have done some further coding. This is a matter of making sure you have consistently applied your coding across all the data you have. In some cases such comparisons may lead you to revise the codes you are using and/or the passages you have coded with them.

Line-by-line coding

An approach recommended by many grounded theorists as a first step is line-by-line coding. This means going through your transcript and naming or coding each line of text, even though the lines may not be complete sentences. The idea is to force analytic thinking whilst keeping you close to the data. One of the dangers of coding, and of any kind of qualitative analysis, is importing your own motives, values and preoccupations into the codes and analytic scheme you construct. If you are not careful, your analysis may more closely reflect your own preconceptions and prejudices than the views of your respondents. One of the advantages of line-by-line coding is that it forces you to pay close attention to what the respondent is actually saying and to construct codes that reflect their experience of the world, not yours or that of any theoretical presupposition you might have. On the other hand, line-by-line coding does not mean you should simply accept your respondents' views of the world. As I have suggested above, try to be more analytic and theoretical in your coding even if this means sometimes that your interpretations differ from that of your participants. Coding should remain grounded in the data in the transcript, but this does not mean it simply reflects respondents' view of things. Looking at the data line by line should stop you 'going native', that is, accepting your respondents' view of the world. You need to reflect that world-view, not accept it.

To illustrate line-by-line coding, consider the short extract in Fig. 4.2. This comes from a longer interview with a homeless man, Sam. (N.B in line 105 I have inserted the word 'term' in square brackets. This was not Sam's word, but it makes it clear what he means by 'long relationships'.) The example shows some initial, line-by-line coding. Some of these codes are still rather descriptive but they reflect the actions that Sam is talking about and some of the ways he sees the world and they prompt some examination of the rest of the transcript for comparisons. Line-by-line coding is just a way to get started and the next step is to develop and refine this coding.

The codes can be grouped in this way:

Relationships – ending	**Relationships – types**	**Friendships**
Domestics	Partnership/relationship	Make friends easily
Relationships a problem	Long-term relationships	Friends geog. limited
Slept in car	Partnerships acceptable	
Break-up		
Mental distress		
Jealousy	**Accommodation**	**Self-perception**
Leave area	Shared accomm.	Chose independence
Avoidance	Peripatetic lifestyle	Characterizes self as
Start again	Hostel seen as live alone	independent
	Never lived on own	Not reliant on others
		Sees self as not reliant

I have omitted some repeated codes and clarified the names of one or two. All this grouping has done is gathered similar codes together. Looking at this grouping and the original transcript, you might begin to refine the codes. For example,

89 INTERVIEWER

90 Have you stayed in hostels for many years?

91 SAM

92 No, err but I've always moved around… since leaving school. I've	*Peripatetic lifestyle*
93 always been in a partnership, err, I've always seemed to. It's been a	*Partnership/relationship*
94 long-term partnership so I've never been sort of out of partnerships	*Long-term relationships*
95 so it's not been too bad. For years and years I've lived with people.	*Partnerships acceptable. Shared accomm.*
96 But when I've had domestics and things like that, well you see, I	*Domestics*
97 left home at fifteen years old and I've never been back to live with	*Chose independence*
98 my mum and dad. I'm one of them sorts of people who don't like	*Characterizes self as independent*
99 going and lying about on friends' couches or putting on people. So	*Not reliant on others*
100 really, yes, if I've had domestics and that, I've gone and slept in	*Domestics*
101 'car – for days on end sometimes. But really this is my first time	*Slept in car*
102 that I've actually come away from everybody and lived by myself.	*Hostel seen as live alone*
103 I have been homeless but I've never had a place by myself. I'm just,	*Never lived on own*
104 like, one of them sorts of people that doesn't like putting on other	*Sees self as not reliant*
105 people. My problem is with me long [term] relationships. I make	*Relationships a problem*
106 friends easy when I'm in relationship. I get a lot of friends but	*Make friends easily*
107 they're friends in that environment and that new place and what	*Friends geog. limited*
109 happens then is I'll break up with her. Me head breaks up and I	*Break up. Mental distress*
110 don't like seeing, sort of seeing other person with someone else. So	*Jealousy*
111 I leave district then and move to another area, so it's starting again	*Leave area. Avoidance*
112 then from scratch, that's what it is.	*Start again*

FIGURE 4.2   Interview extract showing line-by-line coding

there are a lot of codes about the ending of relationships. For Sam, relationships ending following what he called 'domestics' is clearly closely connected with his moving home and homelessness. The code 'Domestics' is what Glaser and Strauss (1967) refer to as an in vivo code. These are concepts used by the participants themselves to organize and conceptualize their world. Notice, though, that these are concepts, not just the respondent's words. In the case of Sam, 'domestics' clearly refers to some kind of argument or dispute with his partner of the time. His use of the term is itself puzzling. It is redolent of police and legal terms like 'domestic violence' and 'domestic disturbance'. Given that Sam tells us later in the interview that he has been to prison, we might therefore wonder whether these break-ups did involve the police and the legal system. In addition, his break-ups also involve some strong emotions like jealousy, so much so that he feels obliged to move out of the area. Notice in line 109 his use of the metaphor 'me head breaks up'. Again, later in the interview he explains how he has also spent some time in a mental hospital, so the distress is severe. Another key aspect of Sam's view of the world illustrated by this coding is his self-perception. Through repetition, he is clearly at some pains to portray himself as independent, not reliant on others and not someone who exploits his friends. Whether this is so is another matter, but he clearly sees himself this way and thinks it important that the interviewer does too.

The next step after this initial line-by-line coding is to refine the actual codes and to rearrange them into a hierarchy. Refining serves two purposes. First, you will need to revisit the text to see whether it is better coded another way, for example using different codes coding longer passages, and whether there are examples elsewhere in the same transcript or in other transcripts that need coding using the new codes. It also provides a chance, as I discussed in the example in Fig 4.1, of making initially descriptive codes more analytic. Rearranging the codes into hierarchy will be discussed in Chapter 6.

Key points

- Coding is a fundamental analytic process for many types of qualitative research. It consists of identifying one or more passages of text that exemplify some thematic idea and linking them with a code, which is a shorthand reference to the thematic idea. Having coded you can retrieve similarly coded text and compare how it varies across cases and with text coded in different ways.

- One of the most important issues of coding it to ensure that they are as analytic and theoretical as possible. You need to move away from codes that are simply descriptive and couched in the respondents' views of the world to codes that suggest new, theoretical or analytic ways of explaining the data.

- For some analysts the process of coding is one that involves the creation of new codes and with that, new analytic and theoretical understanding of your data. They suggest trying, as far as possible, to avoid applying existing frameworks to your data. Others, believing that a complete elimination of presuppositions is impossible, suggest starting with a framework or template of existing codes that reflect current analytic thinking.
- Grounded theory is an important example of a coding approach. The approach has some good suggestions about how to look for passages to code and how to identify the ideas they represent. This amounts to the recommendation to undertake a constant comparison: comparing similarly coded passages with each other, different codes with each other and coding in one case with other cases. A particular technique that grounded theorists suggest, which helps the creation of new codes, is line-by-line coding. Though this approach can be creative, there is still a need to ensure that the coding you come up with does not simply accept the participants' views of the world.

Further reading

These three sources elaborate on the issues discussed in this chapter.

Charmaz, K. (2006) *Constructing Grounded Theory: A Practical Guide Through Qualitative Analysis*. London: Sage.
Coffey, A. and Atkinson, P. (1996) *Making Sense of Qualitative Data Analysis: Complementary Research Strategies*. London: Sage.
Mason, J. (2002) *Qualitative Researching*. London: Sage.

5
Analyzing biographies and narratives

Chapter objectives
After reading this chapter, you should

- know what the analysis of narratives, stories and biographies has added to qualitative research;
- understand the sources and functions of narratives;
- see the particular content and themes of life histories or biographies;
- see these general features of a set of practical approaches to analysis by examination of an example narrative; and
- know more about the structure of narratives.

Narratives

Narration or storytelling is one of the fundamental ways that people organize their understanding of the world (see also Flick, 2007a, 2007b; Kvale, 2007). In stories they make sense to themselves of their past experience and they share that experience with others. So the careful analysis of topics, content, style, context and the telling of narratives will reveal people's understanding of the meanings of key events in their lives or their communities and the cultural contexts in which they live.

Most stories, especially if they are part of a longer interview or dialogue, could have been expressed as a simple example. Rather than the story:

I admit I'm not a good timekeeper, but sometimes being late works out well in the end. I remember the time I was slightly late for a train and thought I would miss it. But, in fact, the train before was so delayed that I caught that. As it made up time, much to the surprise of the people I was meeting, I ended up arriving early.

the respondent could have said:

Sometimes, even if you are late departing you can end up arriving early because you catch an earlier train that has been delayed.

or

Being late is not good, but sometimes you get away with it.

What is added by telling this as a story?

- It provides evidence for the general point (that can be inferred from the particular story).
- It personalizes the generalization. It says, 'I experienced that', which both reinforces the evidence and tells you something about the person, what they feel and how they evaluate and experience the world. By analyzing narratives, stories and biographies we can examine the rhetorical devices that people use and the way they represent and contextualize their experience and personal knowledge.
- The experience is put into a time frame. It is chronological. This is much closer to our experience of the world, which has a temporal coherence to it.
- It acts as evidence for aspects of the self-portrayal or biography being given by the respondent. It gives respondents a voice. It encourages us to take seriously the way people construct and support their identity because through narration people tell us what kind of person they think they are or would like us to think they are. Consequently we may focus on people who are not usually represented or taken seriously.
- It has dramatic and rhetorical force (see Box 5.1). It is easier for the hearer to take on board and it is more convincing and persuasive than the generalization.

Box 5.1   Rhetoric

Rhetoric is the art of making speeches or using language effectively to please or persuade. It arose in Classical Greece, where learning rhetoric was prized as a means to success in public life. Rhetoric examines the methods and means of

(Continued)

(Continued)

communication and has been criticized for considering simply style or appearances ('mere rhetoric'). Aristotle's book on the subject presented a systematization, much developed in later centuries, of the forms of rhetorical argument. This included, for example, the well-known rhetorical question – asked not because an answer is wanted but for rhetorical effect such as to emphasize that even being able to ask it is reprehensible ('How many times do I have to tell you?'). Despite the criticisms that it focuses on form not content, rhetoric is actually just as much concerned with what one could say as how one might say it. Indeed, a basic premise for rhetoric is the indivisibility of means from meaning; *how* one says something conveys meaning as much as *what* one says.

This list illustrates what has been added to qualitative research by the investigation of narrative and biography. It has both focused attention on how people make the points they do, and it gives access to how they wish to portray themselves, how they give account for their actions and their lives. Shared expressions and shared vocabulary and metaphors can tell us a lot about how social groups see themselves and how they account for their experiences (see Box 5.2).

Box 5.2 Metaphors and accounts

Metaphor

Metaphor is the use of imagery as a kind of rhetorical device. Usually a word or phrase that signifies one thing is used to designate another, thus making an implicit comparison, as in 'a sea of troubles' (troubles everywhere, like the vastness of the sea or like storms at sea), 'Life in the fast lane' (a fast and hectic life like being in the fast lane of a motorway) or 'drowning in money' (having too much). Metaphor is a major and indispensable part of our ordinary, conventional way of conceptualizing the world, and our everyday behaviour reflects our metaphorical understanding of experience. Ordinary concrete descriptions are rarely metaphorical, but once people start talking about abstractions or emotions, metaphorical understanding is the norm.

Most of us, most of the time, use standard metaphors that reflect the milieux and culture we live in. As researchers, we can investigate how the metaphors are structured, how they are used and how others understand them. Sometimes metaphor is used because people find it difficult to express themselves without their use or because there is an emotional content to what they are saying that is easier to convey metaphorically. In other cases it is just an example of a shared common term. On the other hand, in some cases the use of specific metaphors reflects shared ideas and concepts among the narrower group to which the respondents belong and are characteristic of the spe cific cultural domain.

(Continued)

(Continued)

Accounts

The examination of accounts can be traced back at least to the work of Mills (1940), who described them as containing vocabularies of motive, and they are also examples of what Austin (1962) referred to as 'doing things with words'. Account giving is the specific use of narrative where people try to account for, justify, excuse, legitimate and so on their actions or their situation. There are two principal types of account: excuses, where people try to mitigate or relieve questionable action or conduct, perhaps by appeal to accident, forces outside their control or lack of information; and justifications, where people try to neutralize or attach positive value to questionable actions or conduct.

Sources of narratives

Texts from a variety of sources can be given a narrative analysis. A principal source is interviews. Rather than go through a predetermined set of questions or even a prepared list of themes, interviewees can simply be encouraged to tell their story. Such elicitations work particularly well if the person is asked to recount their experiences of some turning point in their lives. Typical examples that have been researched include getting divorced, a religious conversion, a change of career, giving birth and getting a life-threatening illness. Interviews are not the only source of material for narrative analysis. Naturally occurring conversations can be used (provided you have overcome the practical and ethical obstacles of recording them) as well as focus groups and all kinds of documentary or written sources, including explicit autobiographies. In some cases you may well refer to documentary sources to support and enrich your narrative interpretations of interviews.

Functions of narrative

Narratives are very common and a very natural way of conveying experience. Paying attention to why people use a narrative or are telling stories at strategic moments in an interview can give an insight into what are important themes for them and suggest ideas for further investigation. Common functions of narrative include the following.

- *To convey news and information* as in stories of personal experience. This is perhaps the most common use of stories and all our conversations are full of such tales.

- *To meet psychological needs*, such as giving people a way to deal with disruptions to everyday routines. These include personal or family problems, financial crises, poor health, changes in employment, or even particularly sensitive or traumatic times or events like divorce or violence. We share a need to restore a sense of order following disruption and we try to make sense of inconsistencies. This process of bringing order is termed 'emplotment' by Ricoeur (1984), to refer to the organizing of a sequence of events into a plot. The sequence can be long or short, but it is important for people to attempt to give it narrative shape. Analysis of the language used in such stories can reveal much about what a narrator feels.

- *To help groups define an issue or their collective stance towards it.* When several people experience an event their narratives can become a common story that expresses their shared experience. An example is coming-out stories told by gays and lesbians.

- *To persuade* (e.g. in a court witness, or a salesman). Such examples use the rhetorical power of narratives and play on the way that they seem to give greater credibility to the report.

- *To present a positive image or to give credibility.* Typical examples here are where a person has triumphed despite early distrust of their views or where their particular knowledge or skills have been important in achieving a goal. Others may try to establish credibility by telling stories showing how their position is the common or normal one.

- *To undertake the social transmission of experience* through, for example, parables, proverbs, moral and mystic tales. Respondents use them to indicate good and bad practice, both to the researcher and to their peers. They have an ethical or moral dimension. A typical example of this is the cautionary tale that recounts accidents or disasters in their organization. Such stories act as a collective reminder of what not to do and how not to be. Moral tales are usually about others, but if the tale is about the narrator this is often because it is an example of overcoming adversity or a key turning point in their life. In many cases, moral tales are a way of passing on cultural heritage or organizational culture, though these functions are also achieved by stories other than moral tales. Examples are atrocity stories, morality fables in organizations, fables of incompetence (such as in medical settings, giving warnings of what not to do), the oral culture of schoolchildren, urban legends, and stories about 'clients' such as customers in retail organizations, medical patients and students in schools and colleges.

- *To structure our ideas of self and to establish and maintain our identity.* This can be achieved at the social level by the kind of moral tales and cultural stories I have just mentioned. Such shared stories can define a subgroup or subculture, especially to those in the group. Being inducted into such groups often includes getting told the key stories for the group. But stories can be used to establish identity at an individual level too. Stories present a narrator's inner reality to the outside world and often it also makes things clear to narrators themselves. We know or discover ourselves and reveal ourselves to others by the stories we tell. As McAdams puts it, 'If you want to know me, then you must know my story, for my story defines who I am. And if I want to know myself, to gain insight into the meaning of my own life, then I too must come to know my own story' (McAdams, 1993, p. 11).

Not every story will perform every function in this list, but stories will perform at least one, and most will have several of these functions. Paying attention to determining the function of the narrative will reveal how narrators portray themselves, what their experience is like and what concerns them.

Narrative and life history

A key example of narrative is the autobiography or life history. Whereas people spontaneously use narratives when telling us about themselves and they regularly include short stories in their discourse, biographies and life histories are usually the result of a specific request. Data can come from interviews, written biography, autobiography, life-history interview, personal letters or diaries.

When giving an account of their whole life, respondents usually order their careers and memories into a series of narrative chronicles, marked by key happenings – the emplotment of the narrative. These can show how the person frames and makes sense of a particular set of experiences. Typical examples of this are how people measure success, how they overcome adversity, what they think of as good and bad practice and explanations of success and failure.

Biographical content

The general approach people take when telling their life history is 'how it happened' or 'how I came to be where I am today'. There are several key features:

- Almost always biographies are chronological. This does not mean that every part of the story is in strict order of occurrence. Sometimes people start 'in the middle' with a key event or experience; however, generally events are recalled in the order that they happened.
- People usually identify key events and key social actors – the characters of their story. These are events and people that have made a difference to them, without which they would not be the people they are now.
- A particular example of a key event is the turning point or what Denzin (1989) refers to as the epiphany, the event that leaves a mark on the person. This is something people say has made them, in their eyes, a different person and they often describe it using terms like 'Before these events I used to do these things

61

(be this kind of person), but now I do different things (or am that kind of person)'. Key events and persons are good indicators of how a person conceives of their life, what it means to them.

- Other common features of life histories include planning, luck and other influences. Often events or people are discussed in these terms – as people whom they were lucky to meet, who influenced them (e.g. partners, spouses, mentors), or as events they had always planned (e.g. getting married, having a family). Such encounters become part of what McAdams (1993) refers to as a 'personal myth'.

Life histories usually have themes and these, along with the features just discussed, can be coded in the usual fashion (discussed in the preceding chapter). Themes vary enormously depending on the person's experience and they may only apply at one stage of the person's biography. Sometimes themes are significant by their absence. The kinds of things to look out for are listed in Box 5.3.

Box 5.3   Common life-history themes

- The relational story – constantly referring to others, what they did with people, to people or people did to them, or in contrast a story where most of the activity is undertaken by the respondent alone. Look for the use of the names of other people and of the pronouns 'he', 'she' and 'they' along with descriptions of actions or look for the use of 'I' along with activities.
- Belonging and separateness – two contrasting themes that may be important for people for whom identity is an issue. Identity, who I am, can be an issue for many people as they progress from being single to forming a relationship and having a family, and then later to adjusting to their children living independently. Issues of identity also arise where the person experiences a fundamental change in what they do, like joining the military, becoming a nun or retiring from paid employment.
- Closeness, remoteness and experience of moving – a theme often expressed in the context of a highly mobile life (either socially or geographically mobile). Typical examples of experiences where you might expect such narratives are the stories of immigrants and those who have moved (e.g. by marriage) from one social class to another. But it might also be a theme for someone trying to break away from what they see as the constraints of family, community or background.
- The idea of career – may be occupational or other social roles, e.g. parent, children, patients. Often a central life concept. Examples include people for whom work is a calling, such as soldiers, priests, nurses, teachers and

(Continued)

(Continued)

journalists, those who define themselves in terms of what they do, 'I'm a full-time mum', and those who have experienced something that has taken over their lives, such as paraplegia following an accident, a life-threatening illness or long-term imprisonment.

- Intimate relations with the opposite sex (or the same sex for lesbians and gay men) – the absence of discussion may be as significant as its inclusion.
- A focus on early life as determinant of later actions – what made me the way I am. This is narrative as a form of account. People are often trying to account for the way things are now – what work they do, what kind of person they are, their relationships – in terms of what happened earlier in their life.

This is an indicative list, not a complete one. You may find in the narratives you are examining that different social, personal or chronological themes are prevalent.

Practical analytic activities

1. Read and re-read the transcript to familiarize yourself with the structure and content of the narrative or narratives. Look for:

   - Events – what happened.
   - Experiences – images, feelings, reactions, meanings.
   - Accounts, explanations, excuses.
   - Narrative – the linguistic and rhetorical form of telling the events, including how the narrator and audience (the researcher) interact, temporal sequencing, characters, emplotment and imagery.

   Look for examples of common content and themes, as listed above.
2. Prepare a short, written summary to identify key features such as the beginning, the middle and the end of the story.
3. Use the right-hand margin of the transcript to note thematic ideas and structural points. Look for transitions between themes. You can examine text on different kinds of transitions such as the move from, for example, professional training to early occupational career. Find text expressive of a particular theme used at specific stages of the biography. For example, is intimate relationship something respondents only mention at certain stages of their life history?
4. Take notes/memos about the ideas you have and use them to highlight where people give accounts for their actions and to show the overall structure of the

story. See if there are episodes that seem to contradict the themes in terms of content, mood or evaluation by the narrator. One special attitude narrators can take to an issue is to fail to mention it.

5. Mark (with pen or pencil) any embedded mini-stories or sub-plots. Use arrows to indicate linkages between elements.

6. Highlight or circle emotive language, imagery, use of metaphors and passages about the narrator's feelings.

7. Code thematic ideas and develop a coding frame. It might be sufficient to use fairly obvious and broad codes like 'childhood', 'professional training', 'early occupational career', 'marriage', 'parenthood', 'national service', 'management', 'career change' and 'retirement'.

8. Later in your analysis, begin to connect the ideas you have developed about the narrative with the broader theoretical literature.

9. Undertake case-by-case comparisons (e.g. thematically). It is likely that you will only have a few life histories to deal with in a study. Even so, some case-by-case comparison may be revealing. You might compare different participants' views on some event they were all involved with or you could compare how people experience similar transitions in their lives.

An example: Mary's separation story

This comes from an interview done as part of a study of the experiences of women who had separated from their husbands. In this case Mary does not give a whole life biography, but starts at the time her husband left her. She tells the story, mainly chronologically, of what happened then and in the succeeding nine years. The interview transcript consists of a series of stories or scenes interspersed with some explanation of events and some description of Mary's feelings and emotional states. The interview is quite long (over 6,000 words) and there is no space here to give a lot of detail. However, I will summarize the text and indicate how Mary's interview exemplifies some of the ideas discussed in this chapter.

Beginning   Mary married in 1963 and separated from her husband in 1994 when she was 51. She has four children, three daughters (one married at the time of the separation) and one son. Mary starts her account with a story of the day her husband suddenly left. She is concerned to explain how this was without warning and that there was nothing in the previous relationship with her husband that indicated he wanted to leave. She supports this theme with several sub-stories such as her son's story of how her husband took all his things with him and her own story of finding, several days later, the house key he had left. An initial issue for her is that of blame. The letter her husband left gave her the impression that she was to blame for the break-up. As Mary put it,

It (the letter) was like you, you, you and I couldn't cope with that really because I thought I must be a really horrible person for that to have happened, you know.

Mary stresses not just how she felt she was to blame for the break-up and how shocked she was – 'I couldn't stay in the house, I couldn't eat, I couldn't do anything, I couldn't function really' – but also how sudden, unexpected and strange was her husband's manner of leaving. She uses the term 'bizarre' several times in the interview to describe the event. There are also several passages where she uses different metaphors to try and describe her feelings at the time. In one she says:

... it was such a shock. I just remember it was like really strong buzzing in my ears and going very, very cold right the way through and I really observed it because it was so bizarre and then the heat followed the cold and came right up my body and seemed to be coming out of my ears and through the top of my head.

Later in the narrative, she admits to having a very visual imagination, and says:

I had this awful feeling of being in the corner of a room with my back up against the corner and my hands holding on and the corner opening. And I'd start to fall through and it was like ... oh God, it was phenomenal because there was only my hands holding on to the wall to stop me. I never fell through but there was something inside me that said if you fall through you'll never get back. You know, I felt as though I was teetering on the edge of, like, a mental breakdown and that was what it was to me this hole opening up in the corner behind me. If I'd gone down there I might have been really, really ill. So it was hanging on to the walls that kept me up really. ...

Not everyone will be quite so imaginative and use such expressive imagery about their feelings and experiences, but passages like this give us very good insight about what it was like to be this person and experience these events.

Middle In Mary's case the latter passage is also part of her transition in the story to a more independent identity. First she recounts how she found out that her husband was with another woman. This began to remove some of the blame and shock she felt. Then she describes an epiphany that happened when, in her distress, she was staying with her daughter and, for lack of spare beds, sleeping with her young granddaughter in her bed. The granddaughter had wet her nappies and these had leaked over Mary.

I think it was then I started to sort of pull myself together ... I had to do something and what I couldn't do was carry on the way I was and be the same person I'd always been. ...

End She then tells how she went on to get some qualifications and then a new career. She also joined a social club for single people and this led to several new and lasting friendships. Then she sorted out her financial circumstances and eventually, at the financially propitious time, she divorced her husband.

What is missing from Mary's account? Of course a major voice that is not present is her ex-husband's, nor are her children's. We only get Mary's memory of what happened. The narrative is therefore from her point of view and what she can remember now. A lot of the story is concerned with showing the listener that her feelings were strong, justified and understandable. Bear in mind that it is quite likely that all the mini-stories she recounts have probably been remembered and told many times before to other audiences. Over such retellings, they will have been refined, re-remembered and recast so that their form changes and is moulded to suit the particular audience. We can see this co-construction of the account in action when, after telling several related stories to reaffirm that her husband gave no warning of his intention to leave, the young, female interviewer was moved to say:

> Looking back do you think there were any things that would have given you any signs as to what was going to happen, or was it completely ...

and was interrupted by Mary saying:

> Completely, completely and utterly out of the blue.

Which she then followed with two stories, one that repeats how calm her husband was just before he left, giving no sign of what he was about to do, and the other about finding out about the woman her husband was now living with.

Mary uses stories to tell the events from her perspective. She uses them to persuade us of what happened, she uses them to illustrate her emotions and feelings. And she uses the narrative overall to show how she overcame the emotional and financial trauma of the separation and, after an epiphany, pulled herself together to such an extent that she now sees herself as a financially secure, emotionally stable and independent person. This is the sense she now makes of what happened.

Narrative genre or structure

As well as examining the thematic content of biographies, we can look at the narrative structure of people's stories. As has been recognized since at least classical antiquity, a story has a beginning, a middle and an end (I used this division in Mary's story) and a logic. Events are not just temporal, they have a causal sequence; one event leads on ineluctably to the next. We can treat the stories people tell as having a plot and categorize them like plays. Table 5.1 gives a four-fold classification of stories based on dramatic themes. I have underlined terms that you might consider setting up codes for.

TABLE 5.1   Dramaturgical classification of stories

Romance	The hero faces a series of *challenges* en route to his/her *goal* and <u>eventual</u> <u>victory</u>.
Comedy	The <u>goal</u> is the <u>restoration of social order</u> and the hero must have the requisite <u>social skills</u> to overcome the <u>hazards</u> that <u>threaten</u> that order.
Tragedy	The hero is <u>defeated</u> by the <u>forces of evil</u> and is <u>ostracized</u> from society.
Satire	A <u>cynical</u> <u>perspective</u> on *social hegemony*.

Mary's narrative falls centrally into the Romance form. Although it starts with a lot of anxiety, financial insecurity and shock at her husband's departure, she soon started to describe how she made a new life for herself. She got training and a new career, joined a social club, developed strategies to overcome the continuing anxiety and came to terms with being in the house on her own. She sues for divorce to get the best financial benefit from her husband's pension. She recognizes these changes:

> The sad thing is that I'm glad now that he went, actually, and that sounds really bizarre because it took a lot of years to get over it, but the changes in me and my lifestyle are so vast now. To go back to that, you know, I couldn't do that.

Life stories progress, they advance or regress, depending whether the story moves on to better things or to worse things, or they stay stable when the 'plot' is steady. If things steadily advance, then the story is said to ascend. Mary's story is clearly ascending. If things progressively worsen, then the story is descending. Others stories may ascend then descend or descend and then ascend as things turn from good to bad or the reverse.

Another well-known classification of stories is one given by Arthur Frank in his book *The Wounded Storyteller* (Frank, 1995). Frank examines the stories told by people who are ill. As he says, 'Stories have to repair the damage that illness has done to the person's sense of where she is in life, and where she may be going. Stories are a way of redrawing maps and finding new destinations' (Frank, 1995, p. 53).

Frank identifies three common story types:

1. *The restitution narrative*. This is the story most favoured by physicians and other medical professionals. The emphasis is on restoring health, the 'me' when I'm better. Such narratives often have three movements. They start with physical misery and social default ('I can't work', 'I can't look after my

family'). The second movement focuses on the remedy, what needed to be done. Finally, the remedy is taken and the narrator describes how physical comfort and social duties are restored. These are often stories told about patients rather than by them, not least because they give the narrator little agency. The patient simply has to 'take the medicine' and get well.

2. *The chaos narrative.* This is really a non-story. There is little narrative drive or sequence, just a list of bad things that will never get better which the narrator is almost overwhelmed by. A typical (non-medical) example is the Holocaust story told by those who survived concentration camps in the Second World War. The story signals a loss or lack of control. Medicine just can't do anything. These are not stories that other people want to hear and they often interrupt to offer good endings such as 'the resilience of the human spirit'. As Frank puts it, modernity (of which scientific medicine is a good example) cannot countenance chaos. It has to have desirable outcomes.

3. *The quest narrative.* This is the teller's story, where the teller is in control of things. Narrators tell how they met the illness 'head on' and sought to use it, to gain something from the experience. This is a very common story told by those in self-help groups. The story is a kind of journey, with a departure (the symptoms are recognized), an initiation (the suffering, mental, physical and social, that the person has experienced, often with reference to the parts of their life that have been interrupted by the illness) and a return (where the narrator is no longer ill but is still marked by the experience). Such stories may contain what Frank refers to as a manifesto. The teller has gained a new voice, a new insight into the experience, and wants others to take it on board.

These classifications overlap with the dramatic forms I gave earlier. For instance, the quest narrative may take on a romance or comedy form. Moreover, as I have suggested by the mention of Holocaust stories, such a classification applies to traumas other than just illness, for instance, legal stories, refugee stories, job loss and separation stories. Indeed you might see many elements in Mary's story as suggesting it is a quest narrative.

Such typologies of narrative structures can be used in a couple of ways:

1. They can be used to draw attention to the way that people portray the events they are talking about. For example, in Mary's case she now sees herself as a strong, independent woman who has found ways to deal with both financial and emotional worries. This always raises the question, why have people chosen to portray themselves that way? Sometimes this question can be answered by examining the content of the biography; sometimes it remains unanswerable. In addition, choosing one type of narrative might require certain issues to be omitted or played down. For example, Mary, in her story, makes little mention of the new partner she is now living with, perhaps because she wants

to stress the challenges that she has overcome rather than the fact that she has managed to re-establish the kind of relationship she lost when her husband left her (Comedy form).

2. If you are examining several biographies, the structures you have found can be used to make comparisons across cases. It may be that everyone telling their story about the issue you are examining (e.g. becoming separated) tells the story with the same structure. This may reveal something about how becoming separated is experienced by people. On the other hand, if there are stories with different structures, then these differences may be associated with other, personal, social or organizational issues that may prove significant in your final analyses.

Narrative elements

Several researchers have focused on the kinds of stories that people introduce into their ordinary discourses, including interviews. Going beyond the simple beginning, middle and end categorization, Labov (1972, 1982; Labov and Waletzky, 1967) suggest that a fully formed story has six elements. (see Table 5.2). By

TABLE 5.2   Labov's narrative elements

Structure	Question
Abstract	Summary. What was this about? Summarizes the point or gives a general proposition which the narrative will exemplify. In interviews, the interviewer's question may perform this function. May be omitted.
Orientation	The time, place, situation, participants of the story. It tells us who, what, when or how, giving the cast, setting, time period, etc. Typical phrases used are 'It was when ... ' or 'That happened to me when I did ... '
Complicating action	The sequence of events, answering the question, then what happened? This is the major account of the events that are central to the story. Labov suggests that these are commonly recalled in the simple past tense. The action can involve turning points, crises or problems, and show how they were dealt with by the narrator.
Evaluation	Answers the question, so what? Gives the significance and meaning of the action, or the attitude of the narrator. Highlights the point of the narrative.
Resolution	What finally happened? The outcome of events or the resolution of the problem. Typical phrases used are, 'So that meant ...' or 'That's why ...'.
Coda	This is an optional section. It marks the end of the story and a return of speech to the present tense or the transition to other narrative.

analyzing narratives and stories in this way to see how they are constructed, we can begin to understand the functions the story performs. The structure helps us understand how people give shape to events, how they make a point, their reaction to events and how they portray them. All of these can be used as a starting point for further exploration and analysis.

Interviews often contain self-contained stories or sub-plots. They stand out from the rest of the responses, partly because they use the past tense and they are often about issues of central concern to respondents, to which they may return at other points in the interview. As we saw in the example of Mary's interview, she tells her biography as a series of short sub-plots or mini-stories. Many of these can be fitted into Labov's structure and doing this helps focus on the sections.

One example is the story of how Mary got a new career (see Table 5.3). This is a simple example, but it illustrates quite well how people tell stories and how they seem, implicitly, to recognize the conventions of how to tell the tale. Not all

TABLE 5.3 Mary's story

Structure	Text
Abstract	Well I had to get some money. I worked. But it just kept me ticking over. Kate (cohabiting daughter) offered to pay more for her keep, but I said 'No it's not your responsibility, I'll sort this one out, I have to.'
Orientation	What I thought was, I'd worked as a social worker for twenty years. I'd retired from that and the one thing that I'd liked about the profession was there was a lot of counselling. I'd had a lot of in-house training for counselling and that was the part that I'd liked the most so I thought I'll do a counselling course.
Complicating action	So I did the RSA1, but it was expensive. I got some help towards the cost of that from the college. Then I did the three-year diploma and used all the money that I'd behind me. The mortgage was going out, everything was being paid. The pension covered that and that was no problem. But I used to have to pay for my learning at Ledbridge and it left me with nothing. But that's what I did.
Evaluation	I came out as a different person totally. You wouldn't have known me if you'd bumped into me in the street, I'd lost three stone in weight and I decided to colour my hair and I turned from a grandma with grandchildren to … into this person that was determined to get on really and make sure she was alright.
Resolution	And that's what I did. It meant I could stand on my own and do a job I really enjoy.
Coda	I'm glad now that he went and gave me that chance to find myself really 'cause I was lost in that family.

stories will fit quite as well into the categories, but most do to a large degree. Looking at those points in their interviews where respondents break into a story, it is quite clear that these are important issues for them. One could almost say that they are defining instances of how they see themselves. Mary told several such stories as part of her overall narrative or biography. One important point this analysis highlights is the evaluation element. This tells you what the respondent feels about the events and, in the case of Mary, it adds more evidence to her overall story of how she fundamentally changed the kind of person she was following her husband's departure. Such stories may also add moral elements to the narrative. Again, in the case of Mary's story, the story illustrates how she has broken away from both emotional and financial reliance on her family.

Key points

- The analysis of narratives and biography adds a new dimension to qualitative research. It focuses not just on what people said and the things and events they describe but on how they said it, why they said it and what they felt and experienced. Narratives thus allow us to share the meaning of their experience for respondents and to give them a voice so that we may come to understand how they experience life.

- People naturally produce narratives and stories in interviews, discussion, focus groups and ordinary conversation. They do so for a variety of reasons. This is partly for the rhetorical and persuasive functions of stories and partly so that experience may be made meaningful by emplotment – ordering it into a sequence of chronicles. Narratives also have social functions as a way to share wisdom and providing guidelines about how to behave.

- In their biographies, people identify key actors and key events that are often turning points or epiphanies. They include a variety of themes, some of which, like belonging, remoteness, career and relations with others, are very common.

- The practical analysis of narrative involves the close reading of the stories. You can use thematic approaches and code them, as in the last chapter. However, writing memos and summaries of the stories is also an important part of analysis. Different people's narratives can be compared case by case.

- Narratives also have a structure that partly reflects the advance or descent of the plot. Key examples of plot are the romance, the comedy, the tragedy and the satire. Shorter sub-plots or mini-stories may also have a structure that highlights the evaluative and affective aspects of narrative.

Further reading

These authors explore the issues of narrative analysis in more detail:

Daiute, C. and Lightfoot, C. (eds) (2004) *Narrative Analysis: Studying the Development of Individuals in Society*. Thousand Oaks, CA: Sage.

Kvale, S. (2007) *Doing Interviews* (Book 2 of *The SAGE Qualitative Research Kit*). London: Sage.

Plummer, K. (2001) *Documents of Life 2: An Invitation to a Critical Humanism*. London: Sage.

Riessman, C.K. (1993) *Narrative Analysis*. Newbury Park, CA: Sage.

6
Comparative analysis

Chapter objectives
After reading this chapter, you should

- see that once you have created a few codes, you can begin to organize them hierarchically;
- know that this is both a practical and an analytic activity;
- see that it also helps with making comparisons, especially using tables;
- understand that tables are a good way of undertaking case-by-case, code against code and chronological comparisons; and
- know that through such comparisons, you can build up a deeper understanding of your data, construct typologies and develop models.

Coding hierarchy

After grouping the codes as I described in Chapter 4, it is only a small step to arrange them into a coding hierarchy. Codes that are similar kinds of things or that are about the same thing are gathered together under the same branch of the hierarchy, as siblings of the same parent (see Box 6.1 for the terminology used to refer to parts of the hierarchy). Rearranging codes into a hierarchy involves thinking about what kinds of things are being coded and what questions are being answered.

Box 6.1   Terms used for parts of a hierarchy

It is slightly confusing, but the way hierarchies are read and arranged is usually downwards with the most general items at the top and the more specific lower down, as in the example on the right. Many people will be familiar with this arrangement from the file and folder (directory) hierarchy in Windows File Explorer. However, we usually refer to the sub-hierarchies as **branches** using the metaphor of a **tree**. A tree is the other way up, with the most general things being at the bottom (in the trunk

or **root**) and more specific, subdivided things higher up in the branches. The two metaphors are mixed because the root in a hierarchy is the top, its beginning. Thus the code 'Evaluation' is the root but is at the top of the hierarchy.

In a hierarchy we often need to refer to the relationships between codes in the same branch. For this we use the language of family relationships. Thus the most general code is referred to as the **parent** and those lower down the hierarchy (in separate branches) are its **children**. Codes in the hierarchy that share the same parent are called **siblings**. Thus 'Evaluation' is the parent of the siblings 'Service' and 'Type of view'. 'Counselling' and 'Careers' are siblings and children of 'Service'.

Branches can be divided into sub-branches to indicate different kinds of things. For example, Strauss and Corbin (1998) suggest that a central part of open coding, the early stage of coding, is identifying properties and dimensions for the codes. For example, in Chapter 4, using the example of coding an interview with Sam, a homeless man, I suggested that codes could be grouped under several headings including 'Relationships – ending'. Some of these codes are to do with the causes of the ending, others about actions during break-up, and yet others about the consequences of break-up. This suggests three sub-branches of 'Relationships – ending', labelled 'Break-up causes', 'Break-up actions' and 'Break-up consequences'. Putting the existing codes under these parents gives

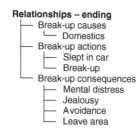

FIGURE 6.1   Organizing a new sub-hierarchy

the sub-hierarchy shown in Fig. 6.1. I omitted one code, 'Relationships a problem', as this is not about relationships ending and probably belongs in a branch of its own as a sibling of 'Relationships – ending'. More ideas that can assist in constructing a code hierarchy are listed in Table 6.1.

TABLE 6.1   Possible types of conceptual relationship between parents and children in a code hierarchy

1. Are types, categories or dimensions of ...
2. Are caused by/causes of ...
3. Affect or constrain ...
4. Happen in these places/locations ...
5. Happen at these times/stages ...
6. Precede (succeed) these ...
7. Are explanations of ...
8. Are consequences of ...
9. Are done by/to these types of person ...
10. Reasons given for ...
11. Duration
12. Attitudes towards ...
13. Are strategies for ...
14. Are examples of the concept of ...

Adapted from Gibbs (2002, p. 139).

Functions of the code hierarchy

Organizing your codes into a hierarchy has several benefits:

1. It keeps things tidy. As your analysis proceeds you may generate a large number of codes. Initially most of these will simply form a list, but some might be in a hierarchy, perhaps because they are derived from an initial theoretical viewpoint. But a long list of codes is not very helpful. It therefore makes sense to move them into a hierarchy where their relationships can be seen more clearly.
2. It can constitute an analysis of the data in itself. In the process of categorizing responses you develop an understanding of respondents' view of the world. For example, in the sub-hierarchy shown in Fig. 6.1 you can see not only that the ending of relationships are important episodes for Sam, but that he sees them as being caused by 'domestics' and leading to various undesirable consequences including distress and homelessness. Of course, others might not see things this way and it is important that you compare these views with those expressed by other respondents. Expand the hierarchy to includes codes for their discussions too, if they raise distinctive issues.
3. It prevents the duplication of codes. This is especially likely where you have large numbers of codes. The hierarchy enables you to spot such duplicates more easily. Usually they can be combined into one code.

4. It helps you to see the range of possible ways things could be (actions, responses, meanings, etc.). This follows the idea in grounded theory that codes or themes have dimensions (see Box 6.2).

5. It makes possible certain types of analytic questions, like did people who did action X in a certain way (talked about it a certain way) also do action Y? Were the characteristics (attributes) of people who did X in certain ways (i.e. that are coded with children of this code) different from those who did it in other ways? These questions lead you to ask questions about the pattern of themes and ideas within cases and to look at the different pattern between cases. I shall examine the mechanics of making such comparisons in the next section.

Box 6.2   Thinking about the properties and dimensions of codes

Strauss recommends that you 'move quickly to dimensions that seem relevant to given words, phrases, etc.' during open coding (Strauss, 1987, p. 30). 'Dimensions' refers to those kinds of properties that can be presented on a continuum. For example, colour has properties like hue, tone, shade, intensity, and shade has dimensions such as dark, light and so on. Typical dimensions include frequency, duration, extent, intensity, amount and manner. What this means is, as you construct a new code, think about the ways in which what it represents could have come about, be changed, affect people, have different types, and so on. Use the list in Table 6.1 to think about what code it might be the child of or, alternatively, what other codes might be its siblings.

For example, in Fig. 6.1 the code 'Break-up causes' only has one child at the moment – 'Domestics'. Thinking about the causes of break-ups might suggest other causes like debt, infidelity, incompatibility, desire for children, changing jobs, and so on. These can be added to the hierarchy, tentatively, and the rest of the data can be examined to see if there are such examples in this respondent or setting, or in others, of text that could be coded to the new codes. Thinking in this way might produce the expanded hierarchy on the right. For the purposes of illustration, these codes are quite descriptive, but there is no reason why you should not undertake similar kinds of thinking about more theoretical or analytic codes.

The dangers of coding and constructing a coding hierarchy

One drawback of developing the code hierarchy I have just described is that you will need to go back to your transcripts to ensure that your new codes are applied consistently to all your data. For that reason it is a good idea to do the kind of development of the hierarchy, and in particular the development of new codes, early on during the coding period.

As you can see from the example in Box 6.2, even with a relatively restricted part of your analysis, it is easy to begin to get a large number of codes. In addition a coding hierarchy can tend to get rather deep (i.e. branches contain many generations). If you are using software that supports such hierarchies, this is not a problem. However, if you use software that does not have such support or if you are doing your analysis by hand, then a very large coding hierarchy will become unwieldy. In this situation there are things you can do:

- Try to transform your codes into more analytic and theoretical ones (in the way I discussed in Chapter 4) and thus reduce the number of codes you have. This will encourage you to move away from descriptive codes, which is often one reason for the proliferation of codes and code hierarchies. In the hierarchy in Box 6.2 you could gather together the codes about the causes of break-up into a smaller set of categories. For example, you might replace all the child codes with two called 'Emotional issues' and 'Economic issues'. What you are doing here is constructing a typology of causes. Do not do this lightly. A typology incorporates an implicit theory or analytic perspective. In the case of the causes of break-up, you are suggesting that they fall into just two types, predominantly emotional and predominantly economic. However, this typology may be useful in your analysis because it might be associated with other differences and variations in the data. For example, you might find that homelessness episodes are more often associated with economic reasons for break-up. (See also the discussion of typologies later in this chapter.)
- Keep your hierarchy shallow. Keep most of the list to two levels (or three if you can't avoid it). This might need some renaming of codes so that a level can be eliminated. For instance, the three-level hierarchy in Box 6.2 can be reduced to two levels by eliminating the root node 'Relationships – ending' and renaming its three children 'Relationship break-up causes', 'Relationship break-up actions' and 'Relationship break-up consequences'. But this is not very tidy, and if you are using software that can easily handle many levels, I would not reduce them in this way.

Comparisons

All too often novice researchers give up their analysis at this point. Having identified the main themes and their subcategories in the transcripts, they go no further. They have identified 'what is going on' and that is enough. A sure sign of this is when the findings chapter of their report is structured in the same way as the codebook, often with sections following the major branches and even the section names reflecting the code names. This may give a clear description of what has been found in the research, but there is still much that can and should be done with the data. In particular we can look for patterns, make comparisons, produce explanations and build models. For all of these the coding hierarchy with its coded text is just a starting point.

For example, we can examine retrieved coded text to look for the ways that things are different and the ways they are similar, and explain why there is variation and why there is not. As Charmaz and Mitchell put it:

> Coding provides the shorthand synthesis for making comparisons between:
>
> 1. different people, objects, scenes, or events (e.g. members' situations, actions, accounts or experiences)
> 2. data from the same people, scenes, objects or type of event (e.g. individuals with themselves at different points in time)
> 3. incident with incident. (Charmaz and Mitchell, 2001, p. 165)

A good way to carry out these kinds of comparisons is using tables. Tables are commonly used in quantitative analysis, where they are usually called cross-tabulations and contain counts or percentages in the cells, usually with row and column totals. They are a convenient way to make comparisons across different subgroups of the dataset and between different attributes of individuals. The tables used in qualitative analysis allow similar comparisons, but they contain text rather than numbers and consequently there are no row and column totals. Qualitative tables are a convenient way to display text from across the whole dataset in a way that makes systematic comparisons easier.

Creating such tables involves retrieving text that has been coded and putting it, or more often summaries of it, into the cells of the table (see Table 6.2). The rows here are two cases, each a respondent in a study. The columns are two of the codes used, one coding what people said about what kinds of people they were friends with (Who are friends) and the other coding text where they talked about their family situation (Family situation). The cells contain a brief summary of what the respondents said that had been linked to these two codes, including in one case a short quotation in the respondent's own words.

Table 6.2 is a very simple example; realistically in a project you will have perhaps dozens of codes and ten or more cases (or respondents). Consequently, the tables will be much larger. It is possible to lay out such tables in a word processor using its table facility. Change the page setup to landscape and use narrow margins and a small font size to get more in (e.g. in MS Word click on **File:**

TABLE 6.2   Example qualitative table: Friends and family

	Who are friends	Family situation
John	Many work friends, one neighbour, ex-colleagues kept in touch with, some from student days.	Lives with wife, two young children (boy 6, boy 3). Employed full-time 12 miles away, commutes by car.
June	Mainly live in the village, neighbours, some old school friends. 'Women I go to the sports club with.'	Divorced, lives alone. No children. Not employed.

Pagesetup... and select **Landscape** in the dialog). Having a large screen helps. If you are using pen and paper, then try to find large sheets of paper to use (like those used in flip charts). Keep cells to a consistent size, that is, make rows about the same height as each other, and columns the same width approximately.

Using tables like Table 6.2 and particularly larger ones, you can make comparisons in two ways. You can compare columns by looking at the text in the cells down one column and compare it with the text in the cells down one or more of the others. Or you can compare rows; look at the text across one row and compare it with the corresponding text in one or more of the other rows. Use these comparisons to look for differences and to find associations. For example:

- these kinds of people tend to act in these ways that are different from the ways others act;
- people in these kinds of situations feel this way whereas those who are not feel differently;
- people who have had certain experiences in the past tend to talk about these kinds of things in ways that are different from those who have not had such experiences.

By inspecting the content of the cells and, if necessary, going back to the original text, you can begin to explain the differences and associations you have discovered.

For example, comparing rows in Table 6.2, we can see how John and June differ markedly in their family situation and somewhat in the kinds of friends they have. Comparing columns when there are just two cases is more limited; however, looking at Table 6.2 you might begin to wonder if there is a relationship between John's and June's family situations and the kind of friends they have.

What cells can contain

Cells can contain a variety of things. The most obvious is direct quotations from respondents taken from the coded text. However, this is rarely helpful because their length would make the table too large and unwieldy. Moreover, too much text means it is hard to make the kind of between-cell comparisons that tables are meant to support. In most cases it is better to sample what respondents are saying and include just brief, salient or representative quotations. Therefore, most commonly, the cells contain your summary or a rephrase in your own words of what is in the coded text. This has the added advantage that it forces you to think about what the text is saying and begin to recognize what is significant about it. As you summarize, try to retain the language of the respondent. The knack is to make the summary long enough to preserve the richness of the original words but at the same time short enough to fit in the cell and to ensure that you do not remain bogged down in the detail of the original text. You can use abbreviations and conventions, but make sure these are agreed on if you are working in a team. Rather than include long quotations from the transcripts, just indicate that there is a vivid passage in the transcript that illustrates the point by using a symbol. Include a cross-reference to the transcript (with page number) so you can find it. Table 6.3 summarizes the various options.

Such rewriting is particularly important if you want to make comparisons between narrative accounts, as suggested in the previous chapter. If you have coded elements or features of the narrative, then just summarize in the way I have suggested above. However, you do not need to have coded your narratives in order to use tables to analyze them. For example, if you have started your analysis by re-expressing and summarizing the stories, trying to highlight the key narrative elements, then you can use this text in your tables. In this way you can use tables to help you compare common narrative elements such as the reference to childhood experiences or the identification of epiphanies between people's narratives.

For many narrative analysts such comparisons are at least dubious, if not irrelevant. For them, the stress in narrative analysis is on identifying the uniqueness of the case and relating the elements of the story in a holistic way in order to understand how the narrator experiences the world. Putting text, even re-expressions of it, into tables breaks up the story and tends to decontextualize its elements. However, I see no reason why narrative accounts that are particular and holistic cannot be combined with case-by-case comparisons. We might, after all, be interested in how different people tell different stories. Each story may tell us something about the narrator, but there is no reason why we cannot try to answer questions like, why are the stories different and is there any relationship between the kind of story and the events and experiences recounted?

Case-by-case comparisons

A common use for tables is to facilitate cross-case comparisons. Cases can be a variety of things. Most often they are respondents or groups of respondents such as families. This will be the case in narrative studies and/or projects using interviews. But the cases can be scenes or settings investigated in a study (such as sports clubs,

TABLE 6.3 What to put in the cells of tables

Possible cell contents	Examples
Short direct quotes, extracts from written-up field notes	Bad experiences. 'When you're by yourself and you're down 'cause you're thinking of things all 'time and your head's muddled up all 'time.'
Summaries, paraphrases or abstracts	Doesn't want to 'put on people', stay in other's homes.
	Homelessness = you haven't got a house or any secure accommod.
Researcher explanations or categorizations	Focus on personalized explans. (bad luck, relationship break-up) rather than structural explanations (unemployment, poverty, prison record).
Ratings or summarized judgements	Self blame – high Level of training undertaken – low.
Combinations of the above	'I don't know how to go about asking people or such, it's not publicized enough ... if it wasn't for hospital bringing me here (the hostel), showing me how to get here, I wouldn't have known what to do. I'd have just been homeless again.'
	Lack skill/information about finding home. (🗐 Sam p. 5)

Adapted from Miles and Huberman (1994, p. 241).

company departments, cruise ships, doctors' surgeries and shops), events (such as football games, Presidential elections, weddings, job interviews and concerts) or activities (such as buying a house, eating meals, travelling, learning to drive and going to clubs). In these examples you may find your text for each case coming from a variety of sources including interviews, ethnographic notes, observations and collected documents. No matter what kind, the cases to be compared should all be of the same type (for example respondents or families or weddings or shops). However, it is possible to make comparisons by respondent and then, with a different selection from your data and a different table, make comparisons by, for example, key events they have taken part in.

For instance, Table 6.4 compares three carers for people with dementia. The first column names the carer, the second gives some brief biographical details. It is usually helpful to include such details about each case in a column. If the cases you are comparing are not respondents but, for example, organizations, then include brief descriptions of them in this column. The second and third columns contain data about the carers' attitudes to care and their contact with other carers taken from text coded with these two codes. The cells contain a combination of selected, representative quotations and researcher's summary.

Table 6.4 is quite small to make it fit into the page and because it is just for illustration. Typically a table of this kind would have many more rows for all the respondents (or cases) in the study and more columns. If you have even a middle-sized list of codes, it will not be possible to include enough columns for them all. You will need to select appropriate subgroups of the codes and perhaps construct a table for each. Repeat the biographical column on each. Typical subgroups include sibling codes in a single branch of the code hierarchy or groups of codes you think might be related in other ways.

Laying the data in tables like this makes it easy to make case-by-case comparisons. Just compare the cells in one row with those in another. By looking for differences and similarities between cases and by comparing with the data in the biography column, you should be able to establish some patterns. Certain kinds of cases tend to be associated with certain kinds of coding. Such tables can also be used to compare columns. One way to do this is to group the text in the cells

TABLE 6.4   Example of a comparison between cases

	Biography	Attitude to care	Contact with other carers
Barry	Cares for wife, Beryl Accountant, Wests, chemical company, now retired. Live together.	No respite care. 'I like her at home.' Not given up much (except holidays) – accommodated activities in life. 'I like to see she's nicely dressed and kept clean.'	Frequent Regular carer from Crossroads (Thurs a.m.) Day care Tues & Thurs Goes to Alzheimer's Society drop-in every Tues. a.m.
Pam	Cares for mother, Denise (divorced 1978) D. in granny flat. Lives with husband and son (17). F/T school-teacher.	Caring is not difficult. 'Because she's pretty even-tempered'. James (son) helps sometimes. Worried if she'd settle when D went to new day centre. 'But she's settled champion.'	Regular Goes to Alzheimer's Society drop-in most Tues. a.m. Some good contacts there. Day care Wed. Crossroads carer Mon. a.m. & Fri. p.m.
Janice	Cares for father, Bill (wife died 1987) Lives in same house, owned by father. Works P/T in bookshop.	Occasional respite care. Gets frustrated when father goes 'wandering'. J misses hill walking with friends. 'We watch too much TV.'	Occasional Day care Wednesdays Alzheimer's Society, been 2X in 3 yrs. Doesn't know other carers.

in a column and thus produce a classification of subtypes. Reordering the rows can help here (see Box 6.3). By looking across the rows it is possible to see if this classification is associated with any pattern in the other columns.

Box 6.3 Partially ordering cases

Miles and Huberman suggest that it is often possible to partially order the cases in tables (Miles and Huberman, 1994, pp. 177–86). This will be particularly appropriate if you have been dimensionalizing your concepts (see Box 6.2). For instance, the last column in Table 6.4, 'Contact with other carers', might be ordered by how much contact there was. I have indicated this with a word at the start of each cell. You can then reorder the rows in the table so that this column is in ascending (or descending) order and bring all rows with the same level of contact together. If you are using a word processor, then use sort on this column to reorder all the rows in the table (e.g. in MS Word select the whole table including the column titles then click **Table:Sort …** . In the dialog, select the column you want to sort from the pull down menu and click **OK**). Alternatively use cut and paste in the word processor to move whole rows up and down the table. Rows with the same dimension in this column will now be grouped together. Now look across to the other columns to see if a pattern appears in them that matches the grouping you have created. If there is, then this might be preliminary evidence for a relationship between the two codes. In the case of Table 6.4, for example, you might expect to find a relationship between the attitude to care and the degree of contact with other carers and care organizations. Successful coping with caring for someone with dementia, indicated by a positive attitude to caring, seems to be associated with combating social isolation of the carer through regular contact with a support group.

Typologies

Using case-by-case comparisons may help you construct some key typologies of your data. A typology is a way of classifying things that can be multidimensional or multifactorial. In other words it may be based on two (or more) distinct categories of things. I suggested a simple example earlier in this chapter in the discussion of reducing the number of codes about causes of break-up. In this case, the typology was developed by examining the dimensions of a code and the cases it is applied to are events (relationship break-ups), not respondents. The key property of a typology is that it divides up all the cases so that each case is assigned to one and only one type. Typologies are useful analytic and explanatory devices, but not every study will produce a typology. However, when used properly, they can help explain key differences in the data.

Ritchie et al. discuss an example based on a study of parents with an adult son or daughter with learning difficulties. The study explored the reasons why the son or daughter continued to live with their parents and suggested a four-fold typology of parents based on their recognition of the need to consider alternative arrangements and the likely immediacy of action. The types were:

- *Evaders*: people who felt 'leaving home' will never have to happen and that their sons or daughters will always be taken care of.
- *Delayers*: people who recognized that action will have to be taken at some stage but felt it was too early or too difficult at the present time.
- *Debaters*: people who felt torn between the need to take action and difficulties of implementing change, but who were trying to begin the process.
- *Action takers*: people who had already taken some action or made a specific plan to find alternative living arrangements for their sons or daughters.

(Ritchie et al., 2003, p. 247)

By using tables like that above to compare coded text, they found that Evaders were probably like that because they had less experience of separation from their son or daughter.

Code and attribute tables

Another use for tables is for cross-case or whole sample comparisons. In such tables the content may come from the whole dataset or from a subsample. Typically, rows and columns are codes, typologies or attributes. An attribute is some property of the cases. For example, if the cases are respondents, then an attribute might be their gender. If the cases were different firms, then an attribute might be the size of the company.

For example, in a study of people who were unemployed and looking for work, respondents adopted different job-searching strategies: routine, haphazard or entrepreneurial. We might want to see how the strategies adopted by women compared with those used by men. Table 6.5 shows the resulting table. Because rows are not cases, cells in this table may contain text taken from more than one case or respondent. It is thus even more important to think carefully about what examples to include and how to summarize them if you give your own explanations. You might need to allow the cells to be bigger than you would in case-by-case tables.

The straightforward way to use Table 6.5 is to ask how gender affected job-searching strategies, that is, to compare the male and female columns. For example, women mentioned childcare and fitting in with working partner's schedule whereas men did not. Before you decide that this is evidence for a true gender difference, you need to eliminate alternative explanations. There might be other factors that explain the difference and you need to go back to the data to

TABLE 6.5   Job-searching strategies by gender

	Female	Male
Routine	My routine's determined by child care requirements (Pauline). I get the paper every day, without fail (June). I used to go down Racetrain a lot, … I also joined Job Club … I kept a file and a record of all the letters I received (Sharon).	I used to spend mornings going through the papers. I either used to buy papers or go down to the library. Afternoons writing off to places for information or filling application forms in, and then evenings for the evening papers, again (Jim). Just the same pattern all through the week (Harry).
Haphazard	Not really, I just do it. It happens (Susan). Not really, because my husband works shift work (Mary).	No routine, but I keep meself busy, like – keep meself occupied – I've plenty of gardening to do (Dave). No, not really. I usually go down and have a look Monday, Wednesday, Friday, something like that (Andy).
Entrepre-neurial	Personal approaches to firms and through friends (June).	I … spend … a couple of days every week with a company. I make sure that they know that I'm there (John).

From Gibbs (2002, p. 191).

check this. For instance, the women might be younger than the men and therefore more likely to have young families and working partners, or it might simply be a matter of how you selected and summarized text for the table.

Chronological comparisons

Tables can also be used for examining relationships within cases. Table 6.6 gives an illustration of this. Here all the information is from a single case, a person with a chronic illness who was interviewed on three separate occasions, months apart, in a piece of biographical research. The rows are significant aspects of their life and the table affords an easy comparison of how their views about these aspects changed (or not) over time.

A chronological comparison is made by reading across each row. Thus we can see how this respondent's views about taking painkillers changed as she became familiar with their use. The same can be done with other rows. However, explanations can be inferred by comparing rows up and down the table. For instance, comparing the text in the cells in rows two and three in columns two and three

85

TABLE 6.6   Example of a comparison within a single case

	First interview	Second interview	Third interview
Pain management	'At first I was worried I might run out of painkillers.'	'I try to avoid taking painkillers because of the side effects.'	'There are times when I find the drowsiness better than the pain.'
Help from relatives	'My husband did his best to help, but he's never done much cooking.'	'Fred went to evening classes on cooking. I think he quite enjoys himself now.'	'I don't know what I'd do if Fred got ill, my children live so far away.'
Independence	'I think I was so self-absorbed with the illness that I didn't worry about getting help.'	'I find it very frustrating having to get Fred or someone else to move and lift things for me.'	'With the new equipment I feel a lot more in control.'

From Gibbs (2002, p. 192).

suggests that notions of independence are not separate from the issue of how relatives help. Having to be cooked for has a clear impact on feelings of dependence in a couple where there was a strict division of labour ('My husband ... never did much cooking').

Models

A model is a framework that attempts to explain what have been identified as key aspects of the phenomenon being studied in terms of a number of other aspects or elements of the situation. Thus you might explain the kinds of friendships maintained by homeless people in terms of their functions (emotional support, drug suppliers, somewhere to stay, social activities) or their causes (through contact in the street, prison, hostel, etc., able to accommodate infrequent contact, emotional needs, etc.).

The explanations you produce when using tables in the ways just described can be fundamental in creating such models. It is from such comparisons, associations and explanations that core models can be constructed and supported. The use of tables in the way I have described suggests that any models produced will have arisen out of a close reading of the data and thus will be closely supported by the data. They are, in that sense, data-driven.

Models in grounded theory

In Chapter 4, I examined some of the suggestions made by grounded theorists about the early stages of coding, open coding. It is in the stages following that, which Strauss and Corbin call axial coding and selective coding, that they

TABLE 6.7   Elements of the axial coding model

Model element	Explanation	Examples from the homeless people study
Causal conditions	What influences the central phenomenon, events, incidences, happenings	Job loss, 'domestics', debt, drug problems, sexual identity
Phenomenon	The central idea, event, happening, incident about which a set of actions or interactions are directed at managing or handling or to which the set of actions is related	Becoming homeless, surviving without a home
Strategies	For addressing the phenomenon; purposeful, goal-oriented	Stay with friends, live rough, seek help from agencies
Context	Locations of events	Hostels for homeless, street culture, temporary accommodation
Intervening conditions	Conditions that shape, facilitate or constrain the strategies that take place within a specific context	Drugs, criminal record, desire to be independent, sexuality
Action/Interaction	Strategies devised to manage, handle, carry out, respond to a phenomenon under a set of perceived conditions	Personal contacts, friendship networks, drug treatment centre, charities, begging, petty crime, move to new area
Consequences	Outcomes or results of action or interaction that result from the strategies	Gets a home, prison, hospital

suggest you should structure your codes into a model (Strauss and Corbin, 1998). Of course, the model must be one that is grounded in the data, and essentially derived inductively from the data. Having refined your coding, rearranged your codebook, compared cases, and so on, Strauss and Corbin suggest creating a model that identifies six types of code. These are listed in Table 6.7 along with a short explanation and a few examples taken from a project on homelessness. The idea is that each element in turn has a causal influence on the next. For instance, the causal conditions produce the phenomenon, which in turn causes the strategies in the contexts. These are mediated by intervening conditions and produce action and interactions that result in consequences.

The final stage, selective coding, involves identifying just one of the coded phenomena or themes that seem to be central in the study. You will recognize them because they are linked to many other elements of your model or because they appear high up in the coding hierarchy. You need to select one of these as the central phenomenon. Even if you have two good candidates, Strauss and Corbin recommend that you select just one. That is often hard to do. The point is that around the central phenomenon you construct a story that brings together most of the elements of your study. Some candidates from the homelessness study are 'becoming homeless' and 'homelessness as dependence'. Becoming homeless, it is clear, is not something that just happens 'overnight'. It is a process that combines several outside (structural) forces with some personal decisions on the part of the homeless person. However, once homeless, people become dependent on others (friends, charities or the state) for somewhere to stay and, if jobless, for someone to provide income for sustenance. This clearly creates a tension as many of the homeless are at some pains to point out how independent they are and how they do not want to rely on others for help. Either 'becoming homeless' or 'homelessness as dependence' could be a central phenomenon, but only one should be chosen as each defines a very different kind of study.

Once you have selected your central phenomenon, selective coding consists in systematically relating it to other codes. This may involve some further refinement in other codes and may require filling out their properties and dimensions. By this stage much of the work you do involves manipulating codes: moving them, creating new ones, amalgamating or dividing them. By this stage most of your activity should be analytic and theoretical.

Key points

- A coding hierarchy arranges codes into groups whereby a parent code may have one or more children codes, which themselves may be parents to other codes. Such an arrangement is useful to keep things tidy and prevent code duplication, but also the categorization it involves can be seen as one step in the analysis of the data.
- Making comparisons is an important stage of analysis, in which you can get beyond the descriptive level. Tables are a helpful way of laying out your data to facilitate such comparisons, although often, given the amount of data you have, you need to consider carefully what you put into the cells of the tables. This can be précis, summaries, key quotations or key words from the coded text.
- A common use for such tables is to enable you to carry out a case-by-case comparison. One key outcome of this can be the creation of a typology of cases based on two or more coding ideas.
- Tables can also be used to compare one set of codes with another. Often it makes best sense if each set of codes is of the same kind and

hence likely to be siblings in the code hierarchy. Another use for tables is to make chronological comparisons; thus you can examine how several cases or respondents have changed over time or over different stages of your research.

- Such comparisons will help you understand the relationship between factors, phenomena, settings, cases, and so on. With this information you may then be able to build a model of the situation that identifies causes, strategies, intervening conditions, actions and consequences.

Further reading

These texts discuss making comparisons in more detail.

Lofland, J., Snow, D., Anderson, L. and Lofland, L.H. (2006) *Analyzing Social Settings: A Guide to Qualitative Observation and Analysis*. Belmont, CA: Wadsworth/Thomson.

Miles, M.B. and Huberman, A.M. (1994) *Qualitative Data Analysis: A Sourcebook of New Methods*. Beverly Hills, CA: Sage.

Ritchie, J., Spencer, L. and O'Connor, W. (2003) 'Carrying out qualitative analysis', in J. Ritchie and J. Lewis (eds), *Qualitative Research Practice: A Guide for Social Science Students and Researchers*. London: Sage, pp. 219–62.

7
Analytic quality and ethics

Chapter objectives
After reading this chapter, you should

- see that the appropriateness of traditional guidelines about research quality, which focus on validity, reliability and generalizability, are disputed in the context of qualitative analysis;
- understand that an underlying issue is the recognition that qualitative researchers, like all scientists, cannot escape the way that their work will, to some degree, reflect the background, milieu and predilections of the researcher; and
- see that this has both practical and ethical implications.

Traditional approaches to quality

Of course it is possible to make a hash of your analysis. You can do it badly or get things wrong. What you describe and what you claim may be warped or biased and bear a questionable relationship to what is actually happening. So how do you make sure this does not apply to you? How do you ensure that your work is of the highest quality?

Many of the ideas about the quality of research have been developed in the context of quantitative research. There has been a strong emphasis here on ensuring the validity, reliability and generalizability of results so that we can be sure about the true causes of the effects observed. Put simply, results are:

- *Valid* if the explanations are really true or accurate and correctly capture what is actually happening.
- *Reliable* if the results are consistent across repeated investigations in different circumstances with different investigators.
- *Generalizable* if they are true for a wide (but specified) range of circumstances beyond those studied in the particular research.

Quantitative researchers have developed a collection of approaches and techniques that are designed to ensure that their results are, as far as possible, valid, reliable and generalizable. However, these rely on things like experimental design, double blind testing and random sampling, things that are inappropriate or rarely used in qualitative research and analysis.

Does this mean that we cannot evaluate the quality of qualitative research? The question has produced a lot of discussion in qualitative research circles about whether there are equivalent techniques to ensure the quality of qualitative research and even whether such ideas can be applied to qualitative data at all.

Validity makes best sense if you are a realist, in which case the attempt to ensure that your analysis is as close as possible to what is really happening is worthwhile. In contrast, for those taking an idealist or constructivist position, there is no simple reality against which to check the analysis, only multiple views or interpretations and hence little point in asking the question in the first place. But even idealists have to accept that although a wide variety of interpretations and descriptions presented by researchers may be possible, some of these will be clearly biased or partial and some may even be downright silly or wrong. There may be no simple, absolute truth, but there can still be error. So the issue of how we ensure good-quality research cannot be escaped (see Kvale, 2007). One response by those undertaking qualitative analysis has been to focus on the possible threats to quality that arise in the process of analysis (see Flick, 2007b). I will examine some of these ideas below, along with some of the suggestions for good practice that might ameliorate the impact of such threats. However, in the last few decades, researchers have identified a more fundamental issue that needs addressing – reflexivity.

Reflexivity

Put simply, reflexivity is the recognition that the product of research inevitably reflects some of the background, milieu and predilections of the researcher. The scientific model claims that good research is objective, accurate and unbiased. However, those who stress the reflexivity of research suggest that no researcher can guarantee such objectivity. The qualitative researcher, like all other researchers, cannot claim to be an objective, authoritative, politically neutral observer standing outside and above the text of their research reports.

Brewer dates these concerns back to Garfinkel and Gouldner (Brewer, 2000, pp. 126–32). Garfinkel showed how social researchers are inside the world they describe and inevitably reflect some of this world, and Gouldner argued that researchers were not value-free but shared values with the rest of their society, and their work therefore had no special legitimacy. Gouldner's point has been taken up and reinforced by feminist writers in the last two decades. They have argued not only that research can only obtain legitimacy by a self-critical focus on procedures for appraising its evaluations, interpretations and conclusions, but that research should concern itself with representation, that is, giving voice to the voiceless, especially in the way research is reported. Such a critique of the possibility of objective science has also been mounted by writers who are anti-realists or postmodernists. For them, it is futile to try to eliminate the effects of the researcher, rather we need to understand these effects and monitor and report them. As Brewer puts it:

> We are encouraged to be reflexive in our account of the research process, the data collected and the way we write up, because reflexivity shows the partial nature of our representations of reality and the multiplicity of competing versions of reality. (Brewer, 2000, p. 129)

The upshot is a focus on what Denzin and Lincoln have called 'validity as reflexive accounting' (Denzin and Lincoln, 1998, p. 278). Researchers, they say, should be explicit about their preconceptions, power relations in the field, the nature of researcher/respondent interaction, how their interpretations and understanding may have changed, and more generally about their underlying epistemology. Suggestions for such an account of the research process that is open to audit by peers are given in Box 7.1.

Box 7.1   Suggestions for reflexive good practice

1. Examine the wider relevance of your project and its setting and the grounds on which empirical generalizations are made, if any, such as establishing the representativeness of the setting, its general features or its function as a special case study with a broader bearing.
2. Discuss the features of your project and its setting that are left unresearched, why you made these choices and what implications for the research findings follow from these decisions.
3. Be explicit about the theoretical framework you are operating within, and the broader values and commitments (political, religious, theoretical and so on) you bring to your work.

(Continued)

(Continued)

4. Critically assess your integrity as researchers and authors, by considering:

   - the grounds on which knowledge claims are being justified (length of fieldwork, the special access negotiated, discussing the extent of the trust and rapport developed with the respondents, and so on);
   - your background and experiences in the setting and topic;
   - your experiences during all stages of the research, especially mentioning the constraints imposed therein;
   - the strengths and weaknesses of your research design and strategy.

5. Critically assess the data, by:

   - discussing the problems that arose during all stages of the research;
   - outlining the grounds on which you developed the categorization system used to interpret the data, identifying clearly whether this is an indigenous one used by respondents themselves (an in vivo concept), or an analyst constructed one, and, if the latter, the grounds that support this;
   - discussing rival explanations and alternative ways of organizing the data;
   - providing sufficient data extracts in the text to allow readers to evaluate the inferences drawn from them and the interpretations made of them;
   - discussing power relations within the research, between researcher(s) and participants and within the research team, in order to establish the effects of class, gender, race and religion on the practice and writing up of the research.

6. Show the complexity of the data, avoiding the suggestion that there is a simple fit between the situation under scrutiny and your theoretical representation of it, by:

   - discussing negative cases that fall outside the general patterns and categories employed to structure your analysis, which often serve to exemplify and support positive cases;
   - showing the multiple and often contradictory descriptions proffered by the respondents themselves;
   - stressing the contextual nature of respondents' accounts and descriptions, and identifying the features that help to structure them.

Adapted from Brewer (2000, pp. 132–3).

Validity

There are several techniques that address the validity or accuracy of the research you undertake – not in the sense that their use will guarantee that your work is a true picture of reality, but rather as ways to eliminate obvious mistakes and to generate a richer set of explanations of your data.

Triangulation

Triangulation gets is name from the principle used in surveying land. In order to get an accurate estimate of the distance of a far-away object, the surveyor constructs a triangle whose base is a measured straight line and then observes the angles between this and the distant object from either end of the base line. With some simple trigonometry, the true distance to the object can be calculated. Using this as a metaphor, a similar rationale has been applied to social research. By getting more than one different view on a subject, an accurate (or more accurate) view of the subject matter can be obtained. These differing views can be based on different:

- *samples and datasets* (chronologically and geographically disparate data and from interviews, observation and documents);
- *investigators* (teams or separate research groups in different places);
- *research methodologies and theories* (ethnography, conversation analysis, grounded theory, feminism, etc.) (Denzin, 1970).

Some writers have challenged the relevance of this to qualitative research. Silverman, for example, rejects this approach since it presupposes that there is a single, underlying reality of which we obtain different views (Silverman, 2000, p. 177). Silverman, like the constructivists, believes that each piece of research will offer its own interpretation of what it finds and it makes no sense to ask which is closer to an underlying reality.

However, whilst triangulation cannot be used in any ultimate sense to create a single, valid and accurate interpretation of reality, there are still practical uses for it:

1. It is always possible to make mistakes in your interpretation and a different view on the situation can illuminate limitations or suggest which of competing versions is more likely. Silverman himself does this when he shows how quantitative data can be used in a qualitative study to reinforce conclusions and suggest fruitful lines of inquiry (Silverman, 2000, pp. 145–7).
2. As we shall see in the next section, there is always a possibility that informants are not consistent in what they say and do. They can change their minds about what they think and say from occasion to occasion, and they may do something different from what they say they do. Forms of data triangulation (e.g. observing actions as well as interviewing respondents) are useful here, not to show that informants are lying or wrong, but to reveal new dimensions of social reality where people do not always act consistently (see Flick, 2007b, for more details).

Respondent validation

As I suggested in Chapter 2, the process of transcription can be seen as a form of translation from one medium to another and inevitably involves some interpretation. What you are trying to do in transcription is to capture faithfully the respondent's view of the world, so one way of checking the accuracy of the transcription is to ask the respondents if you have got it right. Of course you cannot expect respondents to remember, word for word, what they said, but they should be able to pick up any nonsensical interpretations – the kinds of things they could not possibly have said. However, sometimes respondents will disagree with the transcript, even though it is clear from the recording what they really said. This may be for a variety of reasons:

- They have changed their mind.
- They have misremembered.
- There has been a misinterpretation in the transcription.
- Intervening events have altered the situation so they cannot say that in public now.
- They never wanted that said in public in the first place.
- They feel pressure from peers or authority figures to change their opinions.
- They are now embarrassed by having said that.

This raises the question of whether the transcription can ever be a faithful copy of what was said. After all, what was said was in a private conversation, whereas the transcription is, or at least has the possibility of becoming, a public document. These are two very different forms of communication.

You can even go one stage further and give your analysis (or a summary of it) to participants and respondents to see if the account is acceptable, convincing and credible. Of course, in some cases only parts of your analysis will mean much to participants (e.g. a study of children's language acquisition) and in others it might even be dangerous to feed back some of your analysis (e.g. an ethnographic study of militant fundamentalists). Again, there may be a dilemma when participants disagree with parts of your analysis that you think are well supported by the evidence.

So what do you do if respondents disagree? There are two options:

1. You can treat their statements as new data and try to find out why they may have changed their opinion or why they disagree with your analysis. You could treat the transition in opinion as interesting data itself.
2. The interviewee wants their previous statement removed and not used. This is the interviewee's right, especially if you have used a fully informed consent form mentioning the right to withdraw. You have little option but to respect it. You could try to convince the interviewee that the change constitutes valid data itself, and so treat it as the first option. But if you are unsuccessful then you should respect the wishes of the interviewee and destroy the data (see Flick, 2007b).

Constant comparisons

I introduced the idea of constant comparison as a technique in Chapter 4. There I suggested it should be used during the creation of codes and the early coding process as a way of checking both within cases and between cases. In Chapter 6, I considered case-by-case and other higher-level comparisons as a key way of developing analytic ideas about your data. The point about these comparisons is that they are constant; they continue throughout the period of analysis and are used not just to develop theory and explanations but also to increase the richness of description in your analysis and thus ensure that it closely captures what people have told you and what happened.

There are two aspects to this constant process:

- Use the comparisons to check the *consistency and accuracy* of application of your codes, especially as you first develop them. Try to ensure that the passages coded the same way are actually similar. But at the same time keep your eyes open for ways in which they are different. Filling out the detail of what is coded in this way may lead you to further codes and to ideas about what is associated with any variation. This can be seen as a circular or iterative process. Thus, develop your code, check for other occurrences in your data, compare these with the original and then revise your coding (and associated memos) if necessary.

- Look explicitly for *differences and variations* in the activities, experiences, actions and so on that have been coded. In particular, look for variation across cases, settings and events. You might look especially to see how key social and psychological factors affect the phenomena coded. For instance, it might vary by gender (male and female), by age (young, middle-aged, old), attitude (fatalistic, optimistic, self-efficacious, dependent), social background (occupation, social class, housing) or education (private, state, higher).

Two aspects of the constant comparison approach are especially important for validity: comprehensive data treatment and dealing with negative cases. In qualitative analysis you need to keep analyzing the data to check any explanations and generalizations that you wish to make, to ensure that you have not missed anything that might lead you to question their applicability. Essentially this means looking for negative or deviant cases – situations and examples that just do not fit the general points you are trying to make. However, the discovery of negative cases or counter-evidence to a hunch in qualitative analysis does not mean its immediate rejection. You should investigate the negative cases and try to understand why they occurred and what circumstances produced them. As a result you might extend the idea behind the code to include the circumstances of the negative case and thus extend the richness of your coding.

Evidence

A good, reflexive research report will demonstrate clearly how it is grounded in the data collected and interpreted. A key way in which you can do this is by providing the reader with evidence in the form of quotations from your field notes, your interviews or other documentation you have gathered. The inclusion of quotations gives the reader the feel for the aesthetic of the settings and the people you studied. It enables the reader to get closer to the data and enables you to show exactly how the ideas or theories you discuss are expressed by those you have studied. However, quotations need to be kept under control; there are dangers in making them too long or too short.

If quotations are too long

- You use them to make analytic points rather than using your own words. This is, perhaps, the most common misuse of quotations in undergraduate work. It is tantamount to making readers do the analysis for themselves.
- They will include many analytic ideas and the reader will have problems identifying which the quotation is meant to be illustrating. Long quotations will probably need an explanation to tell the reader how to interpret them and how to relate them to your analysis.

If quotations are too short

- They may become decontextualized. You can put the quotation into context in your own text, but then it may hardly be worth including it unless it is showing some particular or unusual use of words (an in vivo concept perhaps).

Box 7.2 summarizes guidelines for including quotations in your report.

Box 7.2   Guidelines for reporting quotations

- The quotes should be related to the general text, e.g. to the respondent's 'lived world' or to your theoretical ideas.
- The quotes should be contextualized, e.g. what question was it a response to, what came before and after (if relevant).
- The quotes should be interpreted. What viewpoint do they support, illuminate, disprove, etc.
- There should be a balance between quotes and text. No more that half the text of any results section or chapter should be quotes.
- The quotes should usually be short. Try breaking up long passages of quotation into smaller ones linked by your own commentary.

(Continued)

(Continued)

- Use only the best quote. Say how many others made the same point. Use several quotes if they illustrate a range of different answers.
- Interview quotes should be rendered in a written style. Except where the details are relevant (e.g. sociolinguistic studies) it is acceptable to tidy up the text, especially in longer excerpts. The full details of hesitations, digressions, dialects and so on can make for very heavy reading. Use (...) to indicate where you have deleted digressions.
- There should be a simple signature system for the editing of the quotes. Say at the end of your report how you edited your quotes (e.g. that you substituted names to preserve anonymity – but obviously not the actual substitutions) and give a list of symbols used for pauses, omissions, etc.

Adapted from Kvale (1996, pp. 266–7).

Reliability

If you are a lone researcher then it will be hard for you to show that your approach is consistent across different researchers and different projects. There are, however, some things you can do to ensure that your analysis is as self-consistent and reliable as it can be.

Transcription checking

One simple thing to do, albeit laborious, is to ensure that any transcriptions you make do not include any obvious mistakes. In Chapter 2, I discussed some of the common problems encountered, especially if you use transcription services. The advice here is simple: check and check again. In the end it is a job you cannot avoid, and in most cases only you can do it. It is very time-consuming, but at least you will get very familiar with your data as you check it.

Definitional drift in coding A particular problem that happens as you build up your coding system, and especially if you have a large dataset, is that material you coded later in a project using codes you established earlier, may be coded slightly differently from material coded at the start. Such 'definitional drift' is a form of inconsistency and you need to guard against it. Obviously, again, constant checking helps. If you have been using constant comparison on your coding, then you are likely to have noticed any developing inconsistencies in your analysis. Another thing you can do to help here is to write memos about your codes. This will enable you to remember later what kind of thinking was behind the idea when you first developed it. Reread these memos later in your coding as part of the checking you do for consistency.

Teams   Many qualitative projects are now undertaken by more than one researcher and sometimes at more than one site. Working in teams can be both a threat and a help to quality. It can be a problem because of the need to co-ordinate disparate work and views, especially if team members have partial views of the data, and differing ideas about analysis.

There are two ways in which the qualitative analyst may operate in such teams:

1. *Using a division of labour.* Different researchers may work on different parts of the project examining different settings or they may take different roles in the project. For instance, one may be co-ordinating and writing, one doing interviews, one undertaking observations and another doing the analysis. The issues here are how to co-ordinate the work being done by these researchers and how to ensure good communication between them. The simple answer is to undertake all the good practice discussed in this chapter and hold regular, documented meetings so that the team can all share in the developing analysis. You need to ensure that all members of the team have good access to all the documentation that the project is producing. These will include all the data being collected along with e-mails, letters, drafts and so on produced by team members, and records of meetings and discussions that are aimed at furthering the research and analysis. If you are using CAQDAS, then this might include giving team members access to the online data and software. If you do this, then consider giving read-only access to the data (or distributing read-only copies of the dataset) to prevent conflicting and unrecorded changes to the analysis.

2. *More than one person engaged in the analysis at once.* Whilst this needs rigorous co-operation to make sure everyone is aware of what others are doing, there can be advantages to sharing the analysis because comparing the work of one analyst against another can be used to avoid bias, detect omissions and ensure consistency.

Code cross-checking

Collaboration on analysis means you can check the work of one researcher against another and thus minimize researcher bias and get a measure of the reliability of coding. For example, you could check the coding of one researcher against the coding of another when both use the same data. This only really makes sense if you already have an agreed set of codes and is a check both on the clarity of the code definitions and how well and consistently the researchers code the text. Inevitably there will be small differences in what particular words or phrases researchers decide to code. Bear in mind that it is often rather arbitrary where coding starts and finishes. More important is the concept or idea that lies behind the code. This is what must be agreed within teams. The concept it represents must be clear and unambiguous and procedures like this may help teams focus on that issue.

Generalizability

As well as using quotations, you can demonstrate how your analysis is grounded in your data by referring to cases and examples in your write-up. However, there are dangers in the way you do this. One is the temptation to over-generalize. It is all too easy to write 'those looking for housing ... ' when what you actually mean is 'one of those looking for housing ... '. You might think the words 'some of' are implicit in the phrase 'those looking for housing', but it will give your reader much more confidence in your analysis if you say 'a small minority' or 'more than half' or even '60 per cent of those looking for housing' (whichever is appropriate). The use of such terms will also help you guard against what has been called 'selective anecdotalism'. This is the use of untypical examples to try to make a general point. It is tempting to pick out exceptionally fascinating or even exotic examples to illustrate your analysis. As Bryman (1988) has pointed out, frequently only a few examples are given in reports so the reader does not know if they are typical and writers seldom give the grounds for their selection. The danger is that you will use exotic but untypical examples to build a more general picture than is warranted. You can guard against this too by using references to frequency.

You need to be cautious about generalizing beyond the groups and settings examined in your project. In a quantitative survey, based on a proper random sampling strategy, you may be able to say that, for example, only 40 per cent of women who were carers got support from organizations compared with 84 per cent of men. As the sample was a proper random sample, you would then generalize from it to the whole population and justifiably claim that men, generally, get more support from organizations than women. However, in the case of qualitative research we rarely have any warrant do this because the sampling is seldom random. More commonly, qualitative sampling is done on a theoretical basis, that is to say, distinct subtypes of individuals are included as representatives of that subtype (e.g. older Asian women) without taking into account the proportion such individuals make up in the general population being studied. They are included because you have reason to believe they may demonstrate some interesting and varied responses. Differences found between groups of individuals tell you something about the effects of those differences, but you should not use the proportions of respondents to generalize to the wider

population.

Ethics of analysis

Ethical practice adds to the quality of your analysis. At the same time, analysis that is poorly executed and badly reported is almost certainly unethical. All research causes some harm or imposes a cost. At the very least it relies on people's goodwill to allow you access to their lives and give you time to interview them. Fortunately, good research may also do some good. It may extend our understanding in ways that are of benefit to people and society, and in particular it may give rise to changes in practice and behaviour that are to everyone's advantage. The key to ethics in research is to minimize the harm or cost and maximize the benefit.

Mason argues that the particular nature of qualitative research and analysis creates two particular circumstances that you need to allow for (Mason, 1996, pp. 166–7). First, qualitative data tend to be rich and detailed, and the confidentiality and privacy of those involved in the research will be hard to maintain. As an investigator you will get the kind of details that only good friends might otherwise hear. This means that the researcher/informant relationship is one of mutual trust and one of some intimacy. It is important that you develop a research practice that reflects this. Two principles that should govern your work here are that you should avoid harming your participants and that your research should produce some positive and identifiable benefit. You might think that any kind of research, even the talking kind that dominates in qualitative research, involves some cost to participants, if only of their time. However, many participants in qualitative research actually enjoy their involvement and get some real benefit from the activity. Nevertheless, in some cases what is being talked about may be stressful or emotionally wearing for participants or in some cases what they tell you may put them at some risk (e.g. from others in the setting who do not want you to know that). So it is not just at the time of data collection that you need to worry about the harm your work might be causing. There are aspects of data analysis too that raise similar issues. Things to consider especially are:

- *Informed consent.* Give informants information about the research that is relevant to their decisions to assist you and do it in a language they are familiar with (i.e. do not get too technical). Get written consent, and if participants are not competent (e.g. young children), obtain consent by proxy. One consequence of this, as I discussed above, is that participants have the right to withdraw at any time, and if you are using respondent validation, they have the right to withdraw what they have said too.
- *Anonymity of transcription.* I discussed some of the techniques for ensuring anonymity in Chapter 2. Ensuring confidentiality and privacy is a particular problem in qualitative analysis because of the richness of data collected. It is an even greater problem with in-house research or studies undertaken at your place of work, where it will be harder to anonymize or hide the details that make respondents and settings identifiable. You might need to make it clear to **101**

people as part of obtaining their informed consent that you are limited in the extent to which you can keep all your data anonymous. People who are close to the setting you are investigating will find it easy to work out who is who and where is where.

This issue involves more than just anonymizing the results you use in your reports. It may be important to ensure that unauthorized people do not get access to your unanonymized data. At the most basic level this might mean not letting friends and colleagues have a look at the original data, and this is especially important if they might talk about it with others so that the information gets back to your respondents and those in the setting you have investigated. More problematic is where you are doing research in an area that is highly contentious or illegal or dangerous, or all three. A colleague of mine has done some work with participants who used to be members of terrorist groups in Northern Ireland. Not only has he had to be very careful about who he has got to do the interviews (someone with the right background whom they would trust), but he has had to be very careful about where he stores the transcripts so that they are safe and secure. It helps that he is not based in Northern Ireland, but even then he has to be cautious about their storage. Of course, it goes without saying that any work he publishes will be well anonymized (unless he has the participant's permission not to).

- *Transcription.* Of course you should ensure that the transcription (of interviews or field notes) is as faithful to the original as you can, but remember also, as I suggested in Chapter 2, that if you employ transcribers, they will get to hear everything too. This means you must be sure that this will not break any confidentiality and that they too may be affected by the content of what they are transcribing. Another issue to think about here is what impression people may gain about participants based on the extracts you quote in your final report. People may have talked in the normal fragmented, hesitant, ungrammatical and often colloquial way they do and you may have gone to some lengths to preserve this in your transcriptions. However, most participants will recognise their own words when they see them (even if anonymized) and some may be upset when they see what they said reported in this literal way. Again, if you are going to do this, it might be worth mentioning it in your fully informed consent information.

Second, in qualitative research it is hard to predict at the start what kinds of things you will find out and what kinds of conclusions you will be able to draw. The study focus may change during analysis and this may produce new ethical dilemmas. As Mason suggests, this means that qualitative researchers need to develop an ethical and politically aware practice to deal with these emergent issues. Some issues this has particular impact on are:

- *Feedback.* You may have offered to give some feedback to participants about the results of your research. You have to do this not only in a way they will be able to understand, but also in a way that demonstrates you have been able to maintain confidentiality and privacy and that their efforts in assisting you has been worthwhile – your work has produced some interesting and valuable results.

However, it is not always that simple. The general principle is that your research should be of some benefit to those involved and perhaps even to the wider society. Problems arise if you are studying people who you do not believe should be benefiting from your work. Those doing research about criminals or hate groups are examples that come directly to mind, although, of course, your own personal and political position might have suggested a wider group of people whom you wish to research but whom you do not want to benefit from your work. Researchers do not always sympathize with those they are researching, such as those who have researched football hooligans and members of the National Front (an extreme, racist political group in the UK).

Another issue that arises when participants see your analysis is that they may feel you have not given their position sufficient weight or credibility. Your research may have investigated a variety of views and you may not feel any theoretical need to give priority or status to any particular one of them. In other words, you are taking a relativist or constructivist view. Your participants may not see it that way, and might feel that what you have said about them underplays their position or is even untrue. One tactic you can use here is to prepare separate reports for different groups that only give details of the specific group they are aimed at. You can reserve your comparative analysis for the less public and more receptive audience in the academic journals.

- *Publication.* Finch (1984) argues that qualitative researchers have a special responsibility to anticipate how others might use their research because of the high degree of trust and confidence generated between researcher and informant. Of particular relevance here are some of the issues of reflexivity I discussed above, such as giving a voice to participants who would otherwise have little chance of expressing their views (although, as I explained above, you may not feel they should have a voice). In addition, particular problems need addressing here if the research is sponsored, especially if the unpredictability of the analysis has an unexpected impact on the interests of sponsors. There have been several cases in recent years in health and crime research where sponsors (governments and police forces included) have been unhappy about the final outcomes of qualitative research. The problem is a difficult one to handle and there are no easy guidelines to follow.

Key points

- Traditional concerns about quality suggest that research should be valid (accurately capture what is happening), be reliable (give consistent results) and be generalizable (true for a wide range of circumstances). But the application of these ideas to qualitative research is difficult and, some argue, even inappropriate.
- Qualitative researchers need to recognize that their work inevitably reflects their background, milieu and predilections. As a consequence it is good practice to be open about such influences and give a clear account of how conclusions and explanations were arrived at. A key aspect of such openness is the presentation of evidence in your reports by the use of quotations.
- Both triangulation and respondent checking can be used to avoid obvious errors or omissions. Triangulation involves the use of multiple and diverse sources of information and, along with checking transcriptions and/or analysis with participants, may suggest new lines of inquiry and novel interpretations. Use constant comparisons to ensure that appropriate variations are accounted for and that coding is consistent (this will also avoid coding definitional drift).
- Working in teams can cause lots of extra problems in co-ordinating the work and consequent analysis, but it does mean that some cross-checking, for example of coding, is possible.
- Avoid the temptations of over-generalization by guarding against selective anecdotalism and by being careful how you make claims about the relevance of your results to wider settings.
- The key to ethics is to balance the harm (even minimal) that research might do against its benefits. Because qualitative data are so detailed, there is always a danger that confidentiality may be breached, so anonymization is especially important.

Further reading

Issues concerning the quality and ethics in qualitative analysis are treated in more detail in the following works:

Flick, U. (2007b) *Managing Quality in Qualitative Research* (Book 8 of *The SAGE Qualitative Research Kit*). London: Sage.

Kvale, S. (2007) *Doing Interviews* (Book 2 of *The SAGE Qualitative Research Kit*). London: Sage.

Marshall, C. and Rossman, G.B. (2006) *Designing Qualitative Research* (4th ed.). London: Sage.

Ryen, A. (2004) 'Ethical issues', in C.F. Seale, G. Gobo, J.F. Gubrium and D. Silverman (eds), *Qualitative Research Practice*. London: Sage pp. 230–47.

Seale, C.F. (1999) *The Quality of Qualitative Research*. London: Sage.

8

Getting started with computer-assisted qualitative data analysis

Chapter objectives
After reading this chapter, you should

- see the development of computer-assisted qualitative analysis software, its advantages and some of its drawbacks;
- know more about three programs, which are considered in detail: Atlas.ti, MAXqda and NVivo;
- have instructions for how to prepare documents, start a project, introduce documents and examine them; and
- see how to carry out coding and retrieve text using the software.

The use of technology has transformed qualitative data analysis in many ways. First, the introduction of mechanical recording equipment changed not just how qualitative data were collected but made possible new ways of analyzing it. The easy ability to get what seems like a complete record of interviews, conversations and suchlike made possible a much closer examination of what was being said and how it was expressed. Narrative, conversation and discourse analysis would all be extremely hard, if not almost impossible, without voice recording. However, since the mid-1980s the technology that has had the most impact on qualitative research has been the personal computer, initially in the development of computer-assisted qualitative data analysis software (CAQDAS) and more recently in the introduction of digital technologies such as digital cameras and digital audio and video.

Programs to assist with the qualitative analysis of data

It is clear from the preceding chapters that carrying out qualitative analysis requires careful and complex management of large amounts of texts, codes, memos, notes, and so on. In fact, one could argue that the prerequisite of really effective qualitative analysis is efficient, consistent and systematic data management. Such a requirement is an ideal job for a computer. The software provides a powerful and structured way of managing all these aspects of analysis. At root a CAQDAS program is a database, although it supports ways of handling text that go well beyond most databases. It enables researchers to keep good records of their hunches, ideas, searches and analyses and gives access to data so that it can be examined and analyzed. However, in much the same way as a word processor will not write meaningful text for you, but makes the process of writing and editing a lot easier, using CAQDAS can make qualitative analysis easier, more accurate, more reliable and more transparent, but the program will never do the reading and thinking for you. CAQDAS has a range of tools for producing reports and summaries, but the interpretation of these is down to you, the researcher.

A key development was the introduction of software that could manage the coding and retrieval of texts combined with sophisticated searching. Such code and retrieve programs not only make it easy to select chunks of text (or even parts of images) and apply codes to them, but they also make it easy to retrieve all similarly coded text without decontextualisation, that is, without losing any information about where that text came from. More recently, some CAQDAS tries to assist with analytic procedures too. The programs provide a variety of facilities to help the analyst examine features and relationships in the texts. They are often referred to as theory builders – not, it should be noted, because on their own they can build theory, but because they contain various tools that assist researchers to develop theoretical ideas, make comparisons and test hypotheses.

Dangers of CAQDAS

Whilst there are many benefits to be gained from using CAQDAS, there are dangers too. Fielding and Lee (1998) discuss some of these in their book. Here they examine the history of the development of qualitative research and its support by computers in the light of the experience of those interviewed in their study of researchers using CAQDAS. Amongst the issues they identify is a feeling of being distant from the data. Researchers using paper-based analysis felt they were closer to the words of their respondents or to their field notes than if they used computers. This is probably because many of the early programs did not make it easy to jump back to the data to examine the context of coded or retrieved text. In contrast, recent programs excel at this. A second issue, as many users and some commentators have suggested, is that much software seems too influenced by grounded theory. This approach, discussed in Chapters 4 and 6, has become very popular amongst both qualitative researchers and software developers. However, as Fielding and Lee point out, as programs have become more sophisticated, they have become less connected to any one analytic approach. A related danger that some have pointed to is the over-emphasis on code and retrieve approaches. Indeed, these are core activities of CAQDAS. Some commentators have suggested that this militates against analysts who wish to use quite different techniques (such as hyperlinking) to analyze their data. But it is clear that coding is central in the kind of analysis best supported by most CAQDAS, and although some software does have linking facilities, these are not as well developed as those that support coding.

Features of the programs

Despite the prevalence of code and retrieve functions in CAQDAS, there remain distinct differences in approach between programs. We are nowhere near the situation in word processing where one program dominates the market. Some programs are better at some kinds of analysis and better for some purposes than others. If you are able to choose what software to use before you start analysis, then it is important to know which is good at what. One place to start is the websites run by the publishers of the software. They often have demonstration versions of the program that you can download to try out. Typically these do not allow saves or are limited to a number of runs.

At the time of writing three programs seem to be the most frequently used by researchers, and many of them are available to students through university networks. They are Atlas.ti, now in version 5; MAXqda v.2, the latest version of a program that started life as WinMax; and NVivo, now in version 7, which is a development of the company's original program, Nud.ist. As you will see from what follows, all three share very similar features:

- import and display rich texts;
- the construction of code lists, in most cases as a hierarchy;
- retrieval of text that has been coded;
- the examination of coded text in the context of the original documents;
- the writing of memos that can be linked to codes and documents.

There are, however, differences. MAXqda and NVivo have the simplest support for hierarchical coding, though Atlas.ti supports hierarchies through its network facility. All the programs can import and edit rich text files and can code down to a single word. MAXqda is probably the easiest to learn and has the most approachable interface. All the programs have very strong search functions, with

NVivo having probably the most powerful as it includes matrix searching of a kind that can support the use of tables for comparisons (as discussed in the last chapter). All three programs include very flexible networking or charting features. In all programs, items in the charts are directly linked to the qualitative codes and data, and Atlas.ti comes with a built-in set of logical relationships that are directly tied to the analysis.

The rest of this chapter will go through the basic functions of these three programs, reflecting the kinds of analysis discussed in the previous chapters. This will show how to set up a project, how to introduce documents to be analyzed and how to do some simple coding and retrieval. The next chapter will examine perhaps the most important of the tools in CAQDAS programs, search. Instructions for each of the basic functions will be given for each program and these will be distinguished by the use of these icons:

Atlas.ti: MAXqda: NVivo:

In the instructions the following symbols and conventions are used:

☞ means click on the menu, button, etc., with the left mouse button.

☞ means click on the item with the right mouse button and use the contextual menu. This is a very useful feature of the programs. Most objects in the programs, like documents, text, codes, and so on, have an associated pop-up menu that contains the most frequently used functions associated with that object. In fact, many functions can be selected in one of four ways: menu bar, toolbar icon, keyboard shortcut or context-sensitive pop-up menu. As you become familiar with your program you will find yourself using a combination of these methods best suited to your own style.

☞ means double-click on the item with the left mouse button.

Menu items, button names and other items to be clicked are shown in bold. Hierarchical menus are shown with colons between the levels. Thus ☞ **Edit:Copy** means select the item 'Copy' from the 'Edit' menu.

Preparing the data for introduction into the project

In Chapter 2, I discussed the issues of transcription and preparing electronic files for analysis and suggested some of the ways to lay out the file. In addition to those recommendations there are some further guidelines to bear in mind when using these three programs. All the programs accept files in plain text format, but they also accept rich text format and work better with such files. (see Box 8.1). Some can import MS Word .doc files, but work better with rich text format.

Box 8.1 Plain text and RTF

Plain text

This is a minimal standard. It does not include information on different fonts, colours, font sizes, bold, italic and roman text and line justification. Plain text includes only characters and a limited range of punctuation marks and symbols. This uses a .txt extension.

Rich text format (RTF)

This format allows you to retain different fonts, colours, font sizes, bold, italic and roman text and certain aspects of layout such as how lines are justified. It is best to do all this formatting work in your word processor before introducing the files into the program. In the word processor, save the files as type RTF. (In MS Word this is an option in the pull-down menu at the bottom of the Save As dialog and gives the file an.rtf extension.) In an RTF file, words in a paragraph wrap to match the available space. There are carriage returns only at the end of paragraphs. Some programs do not always handle some of the more complex RTF features very well (e.g. tables). It is best to experiment first with a few such files before your final import of them into your project.

Microsoft Word documents (.doc)

This format allows all the formatting and features that RTF does and a lot more, specific to the Word program. Though some programs can import .doc files, it is usually best to save them as RTF before importing. There are many facilities like footnotes and cross-referencing that cannot be handled by the CAQDAS programs and these are best left out of your documents if possible.

Atlas.ti. The latest version of this program accepts RTF files. However, in Atlas.ti, paragraphs can be grouped. The end of a group of paragraphs is indicated by two carriage returns. This is important if you want to use the autocode features where it is possible to select a paragraph group as the quotation to be linked to the code. For example, in an interview with a respondent you might put two carriage returns at the end of each respondent response and use single returns elsewhere.

MAXqda. Can also accept RTF files.

NViVO. Accepts RTF files. The program also recognizes sections and parts of the file using paragraph styles. These are the same as styles in MS Word and, with one exception, use default MS Word styles. Sections are indicated by the use of the heading styles: Heading 1, Heading 2, etc. A section starts at a paragraph in one of the heading styles and ends at the start of the next paragraph that is in a heading style. Sections like this make possible the autocoding of documents in NVivo. A common practice here is to put the name of the speaker in its own paragraph and give it a heading style. Again, the search tool can spread finds to the enclosing section and code it to the new code created.

General points

- When saving files as RTF, make sure that you use normal margins and single spacing (even though you may have done otherwise when printing out the transcripts).
- Always make spelling, spacing, etc., of repeating speaker identifiers, question headers, section headers and topic headers consistent throughout the text, e.g. QU1: or Q1:, not a mixture of both. You may need to depend on this uniformity when performing text searches. It is easier to use text search tools that look for exact strings of characters, not approximations. Lay out the file in a neat manner, for example by putting the speaker's name (or identification) in capitals and then type a colon or tab before the actual text. It is normal to keep the speaker's name on the same line as the text that follows, However, if you are using NVivo, and you put the speaker's name on a line of its own (i.e. in its own paragraph), you can give it a heading style that will indicate a section break to the program and that can be used in certain searches and automatic coding options. Put two carriage returns before each speaker as this makes the transcript easier to read (both online and when printed). If you are using Atlas.ti, two carriage returns can be used to indicate a paragraph break that is significant when doing automatic coding. In that case you may, for example, want to restrict the use of two carriage returns to the start of each pair of interviewer question and respondent answer.
- If possible, before transcribing too much data, prepare a small pilot project with one or two files, using the CAQDAS program. Do some coding and retrieval, and text searches, to test that the formatting of the data seems to work.

New project

When you start your program for the first time, you will be asked if you want to use an existing project (called a hermeneutic unit in Atlas.ti) or create a new one.

(You may also have the option to open a tutorial file at this point.) ⬉ the program's icon to start it or select it from the **Start:Programs** pop-up menu, then:

 Atlas.ti

The **Welcome dialog** appears. ✓ **Create a new Hermeneutic Unit**. ✓ **OK**. The main Atlas.ti workbench window opens. This stays open and gives access through buttons and menus to the functions of Atlas.ti (see Fig 8.1). This shows a primary text open (the interview with Barry examined in Chapter 4) and some coding. The lines coded are indicated with a coloured bracket and the name of the associated code shows in line with the top of the bracket and in the same colour. Clicking on the bracket or the name of the code will highlight the actual words coded – called a quotation. Each of the pull-down list menus (documents, quotations, codes, memos) has an associated button, which opens a list manager window.

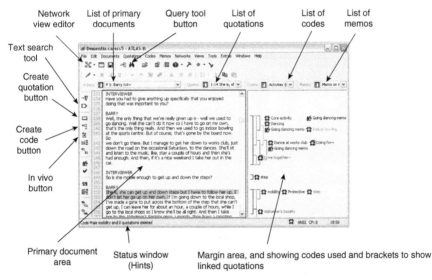

FIGURE 8.1 Atlas.ti workbench window

M MAXqda

The Open Project dialog appears. ✓ **Create and Open New Project**. ✓ **OK** In the New Project dialog, name your project, ✓ **Open**. The MAXqda desktop opens (see Fig. 8.2). There are four panes, Document System, Text Browser,

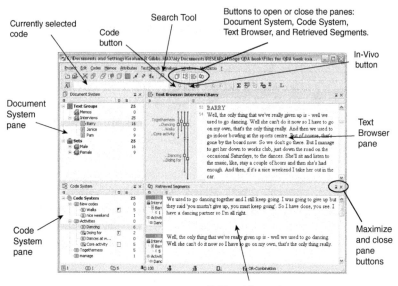

Currently selected code

Code button

Search Tool

Buttons to open or close the panes: Document System, Code System, Text Browser, and Retrieved Segments.

In-Vivo button

Document System pane

Text Browser pane

Code System pane

Maximize and close pane buttons

Retrieved Segments pane

FIGURE 8.2 The MAXqda Desktop window

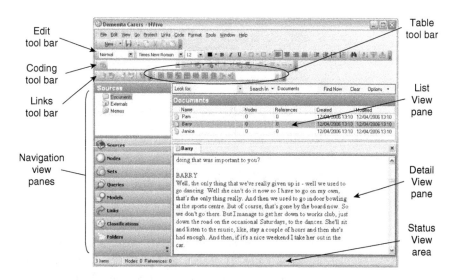

Edit tool bar

Coding tool bar

Links tool bar

Navigation view panes

Table tool bar

List View pane

Detail View pane

Status View area

FIGURE 8.3 The NVivo main window

Code System and Retrieved Segments. The panes can be displayed and hidden independently and can also be expanded to the whole window.

 NVivo7   The Welcome screen appears. 🖘 New Project button. The New Project dialog is displayed. Give your project a name in the Title field and description if you want. 🖘 the Browse button to chose where you want to save your project file then 🖘 **OK**. The main NVivo window opens with the name of your new project in the title bar (see Fig. 8.3).

Backing up and security

As you build your project and develop your analysis, you will create files and structures you will not want to lose. Do regular saves of your data. In addition some programs do regular automatic saves of your data or produce backup files, so that if the program or the computer crashes at any time, you will not lose all your work.

Most of the data you create is very compact. Information about codes and links takes only a little space. But your documents and reports will take up lots of space and you may well find all the files are too large to fit onto a floppy disk. Besides, floppy disks are not a safe medium. They easily corrupt. I recommend the use of a compact flash card or a lightweight removable hard drive for backing up. However, any high-capacity removable storage device will do, including rewritable CD-ROM or DVD. Even though modern hard disks are very reliable, never rely on just one copy. Hard disks can fail. Your computer may be stolen or someone may accidentally delete your files. After months of working on your project you do not want to lose all your work.

As well as ensuring you do not lose your data, you need to ensure that unauthorized people do not get access to it. This is particularly important if you have given undertakings of anonymity to participants. No one outside the trusted members of your research group should have access to the real identity of your participants and the settings and organizations they operate in. Whilst you may be used to keeping paper copies of such information under lock and key, you might be less careful about electronic copies of it. It is not necessary to go to the lengths of encrypting all your files, but using a password on your computer and on your CAQDAS program project are wise acts – and do not keep the password written on a scrap of paper attached to the monitor. Think also about the final disposal of the data. At the end of a project, when all publications have been finished, consider archiving all your data onto CD-ROM or DVD (at least two copies) and then keep them locked up somewhere safe. You can then delete all the data held elsewhere (e.g. on hard disks). Physically destroy unwanted copies of the data stored on CD-ROMs and floppy disks. It might even be worth buying a special program to overwrite deleted copies of the data on your hard disks or memory sticks. (Deleting on the computer does not actually delete the data, it just removes the reference to it.)

Documents

Fundamentally, the three programs all do two basic things. They support the storing and manipulation of texts or documents and they support the creation and manipulation of codes. (NVivo and Atlas.ti also allow you to link to images, sounds and video, and Atlas.ti allows you to code these too.) Around these two basic functions the programs also provide tools for creating and examining new ideas about the data (e.g. through searching, writing memos and charting) and for retrieving and reporting results.

Introducing new, transcribed documents into the programs

When you start a new project there are two things you can do: introduce your transcribed documents (including any memos you have already written) or set up your coding system. Of course, if you are following an inductive, exploratory approach to data analysis, you will need to introduce and read the documents before you come up with any coding. However, if you are basing your coding at least on some prior theory and research, then you can enter codes into the project without initially any documents to work on. The documents can be added later. In most cases, however, you will probably want to work on documents and generate some, if not all, your codes from them.

Atlas.ti — ✔ **Documents:Assign**. In the file selector dialog find and select the file you want to assign (introduce) to your HU. ✔ **Open**. The file name appears in the pop-down menu of primary documents. Selecting it from this menu will display its contents.

MAXqda — In the **Document System** pane ⬙ **Text Groups,** ✔ **New Text Group**. Type a name (e.g. Interviews). ⬙ this Text Group name, ✔ **Import Text(s)**. In the file selector dialog find and select the files you want to import (introduce). ✔ **Open**. Like the code system, the document system is hierarchical. ✔ the plus and minus signs to open and close the hierarchy.

NVivo — In the Navigation View pane ✔ **Sources.** In the Sources pane ✔ the **Documents** folder. ⬙ in the List view pane and ✔ **Import Documents ...** The Import Documents dialog opens. 🖎 **Browse** button. In the file selector dialog that opens, find and select the file(s) you want to import (introduce) into your project. 🖎 **Open** and in the Import Source(s) dialog 🖎 **OK**.

Examining documents

Once you have introduced files they stay as part of the project. You can examine them at any time.

 Atlas.ti   🖎 on the Primary document pop-down menu (see Fig 8.4), 🖎 the document you want to display. The document appears in the primary document area.

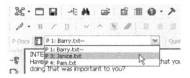

FIGURE 8.4   The Atlas.ti Primary document pop-down menu

MAXqda   In the Document System pane 🖎 the name of the document you want to display (or drag it to the Text Browser pane) its contents appear in the Text Browser pane. In the Document System pane the icon changes to a text with a pencil.

NVivo   In the Navigation View pane 🖎 **Sources.** In the **Sources** pane 🖎 **Documents** folder. The list of documents appears in the List view pane. 🖎 the name of the document you wish to display. It opens in a Detail view pane below the list or to its right.

Coding

I discussed the processes of coding in Chapter 4. There I suggested it is possible to establish codes without any reference to the text, which suits the situation where you have a good idea before analyzing the data about what kinds of phenomena and concepts you are likely to find. You can then select sections of text and assign or link them to these a priori codes. On the other hand, all the programs also support developing coding directly from the text, where you select some text and then assign a new or existing code to it.

In Atlas.ti, the Quotation and the Code lists and pop-up menus support coding. Codes can also be arranged into families or groups. In Atlas.ti, codes (as well as documents, quotations and memos) can be linked to each other in networks. In a network view, codes can be arranged hierarchically or in any other way. The linkages are named, for example, 'is part of' or 'contradicts' in the case of codes or 'criticizes' or 'justifies' in the case of quotations. Codes, quotations, documents, and so on can be displayed in a Windows Explorer fashion in the Object Explorer.

Coding in MAXqda is supported by the Code System pane. All codes in MAXqda are hierarchically arranged. As a temporary measure, if you do not know where in the rest of the hierarchy to put new codes, you can create a parent, placeholder code called 'New Codes' and keep them as its children as you create them. Move them elsewhere in the hierarchy later.

NVivo calls codes 'nodes' and distinguish free nodes and tree nodes. Typically when you first create a node it is a free node that is just kept in a list. Tree nodes have all the properties of free nodes, but in addition they are organized into a hierarchy or tree shown in the node list view pane. Free nodes can be made into tree nodes (and vice versa).

In each program you can create, delete, merge and move codes and change the text to which they refer. At any time you can browse or display the coded text, change the coding or view the coding in context. This makes the process of coding a lot more flexible than when using paper. You can do some rough coding, perhaps using the text search tool (see the next chapter) and then review and revise what you have done. You can change the text that is coded, expanding it or reducing it as you see fit. You can code additional passages to existing codes as you come across them. It is also possible to divide up coded material if, for example, you decide that material coded by one code actually represents two different thematic ideas. Codes can also be searched and in this way, along with an inspection of linked data, like memos, the researcher can ask questions of the data and build and test theories. This will be examined in more detail in the next chapter.

Creating a new code

Use this approach where you want to create codes without referring to the text, perhaps because you are guided by some existing theory or expectations as to what you expect to find. As you create codes (by whatever approach) do not forget to keep a record, either as a comment or in a memo (both can be stored in the project files), of what the code represents and what your thinking about it is.

 Atlas.ti ✔**Codes: Create Free Code**. In the Free Code(s) dialog type a name, ✔ **OK**. A code with no text coded to it is created.

MAXqda

In the Code System window, ➘ the name of a code you want to be the new code's parent, ✔ **New Code.** Type in a name.

NVivo

In the Navigation View pane ✔ **Nodes.** ✔ **Free Nodes** folder. In the main toolbar ✔ **New** button. (The pop-up menu changes depending on the context.) ✔ **Free Node in this Folder**. Type in a name and optional description and ✔ **OK**.

If you wish to create a tree node and you have already created some branches, then in the Navigation View pane ✔ **Nodes** then ✔ **Tree Nodes** folder to see the existing nodes. ➘ the name of a node in the list view pane that you want to be the new code's parent (see Fig 8.5). ✔ **Add Tree Nodes** ... and type in a name, etc.

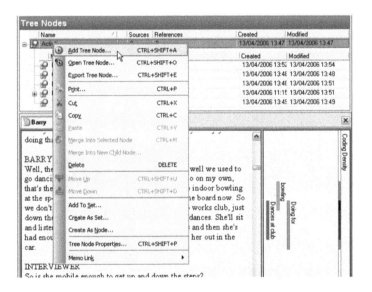

FIGURE 8.5   Creating a new tree node in NVIvo using the pop-up menu

Using existing codes for coding

This is the most common situation, where you have developed a lot of codes and are simply working through the documents coding their contents. You read the text and identify a passage as being about some theme you already have a code for.

Atlas.ti | Select the text you want to code in the primary text area. ⬛ in the selected text, ✔ **Coding:Code by List**. ✔ the code you want in the list window. ✔ **OK**. Or, select the text then drag the code you want from the Codes Manager window onto the selected text.

MAXqda | Select the text you want to code in the Text Browser. Drag the selected text from the Code System window onto the code name. Or, if the code name you want is already highlighted in the toolbar (or you can choose it from the pull-down list), ✔ the Coding with Quicklist button (✱) in the toolbar.

NVivo | In the document find and select the text you want to code. ✔ **Nodes** and then ✔ **Free Nodes** or **Tree Nodes** in the Navigation view pane to display the required nodes in the List view pane. Drag the selected text to the required node. (You may find it easier to rearrange the view so that you can display a longer list of nodes. ✔ **View:Detail view: Right**.)

Creating new codes from the transcripts

You do this when you are following the inductive approach. You read the text, identify a theme or some content that can be coded, and create a new code for it and code the text immediately.

Atlas.ti | In Atlas.ti this is called open coding. Select the text you want to code in the primary document text area. ✔ Open Coding button (⊐) in the left-hand button bar. An open coding dialog opens. Type in the name of the code. ✔ **OK**.

MAXqda | If you select just a word or short phrase in the Text Browser you can code it in vivo. ✔ the In-Vivo-Coding button (✱) in the toolbar. Otherwise you must have already created a code. Select the text you want to code in the Text Browser. Drag the selected text onto the code name in the Code System pane.

NVivo | Select the text you want to code in the detail view pane. ✔ **Code** menu, ✔ **Code:Code Selection at New Node ...** The New Node dialog is opened. ✔ **Select** button. In the Select Location dialog that is displayed, ✔ **Folders** in the left panel, ✔ **Free Node** in the right panel and ✔ OK. Enter a name in the Name field and an optional description. ✔ **OK**.

Examining existing codes

Once you have created some codes and/or done some coding, use this approach to explore what codes you have created.

Atlas.ti   If a primary text is displayed, then codes can be seen in the Margin area (if not displayed, ✔ **Views:Margin Area**). To list codes ✔ Codes Manager button ▣ or ✔ **Codes:Code Manager**. The Code Manager window opens. The area at the bottom is for a brief comment or description of the selected code.

MAXqda   Codes are listed in the Code System pane (see Fig 8.6). ✔ the plus signs or the minus signs to expand or collapse the hierarchy.

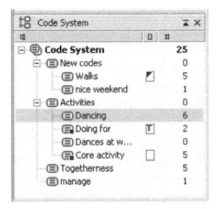

FIGURE 8.6   MAXqda Code System pane

NVivo   Nodes are listed in the list view pane. ✔ **Nodes** and then ✔ **Free Nodes** or **Tree Nodes** in the Navigation view pane. In the case of tree nodes, ✔ the plus signs or the minus signs to expand or collapse the hierarchy in the list view.

Displaying the coded text in context

With some text coded you can inspect the documents to see how they are coded. This is a most important process in re-contextualizing your coding. All three programs use coding stripes to show what lines are coded. By clicking on the stripe you will highlight the text so you can see the exact words that are coded. Thus you can see the context in which the coded text appears and, if you wish, you can extend or reduce the amount of text coded.

119

Atlas.ti

For any document displayed, Atlas.ti always shows the associated coding in the margin area. If it is not displayed ✔ **Views:Margin Area**. Click on a coding bracket to show exactly what text is coded (see Fig. 8.7).

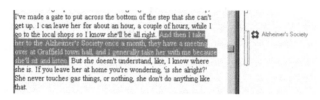

FIGURE 8.7   Selected quotation bracket showing text in the quotation

 MAXqda

When a document is displayed in the Text Browser, any coding shows in the code column to the left. ✔ the coding bar to see exactly what text is coded (see Fig 8.8)

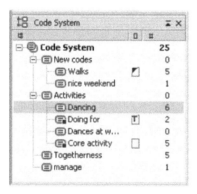

FIGURE 8.8   Selected coding bar showing coded text

NVivo

Open the document you want to examine in the Detail view pane. ✔ **View:Coding Stripes**. ✔ the required display option. (Most coding and Recently coding are useful options.) If your option includes more than 7 nodes, you will have to select just 7 from a Select Project Items dialog. Coding stripes are shown in a panel to the left of the text (see Fig 8.9). ✔ the coding stripe to see exactly what text is coded (highlighted in ochre).

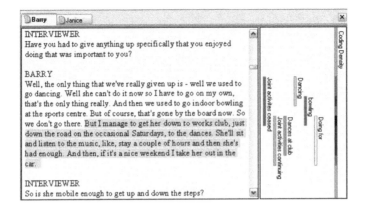

FIGURE 8.9   Document showing coding stripes

Retrievals

Having done some coding you will want to examine all the text you have coded with a particular code. The process is called retrieval. The retrieved text tells you about the ways that all participants in your study were talking about the particular theme the code represents. It is therefore a key function in supporting constant comparison (see Chapter 4) and thus contributing to the quality of your analysis (see Chapter 7). The text can be cut and pasted to your word processor to use for quotations in your final write-up.

 Atlas.ti   Open the Codes list window. ☝ the code you want to retrieve, ✔ **Output:Quotations for Selected Code**. ✔ **Yes**, to include comments. ✔ **Editor**. An edit window opens with a document listing all the quotations for the selected code with any comments. This can be saved or printed. The contents can be cut and pasted to your word processor.

 MAXqda   Activate all the documents you want to retrieve from (e.g. ☝ the text group name in the Document System pane, ✔ **Activate All Texts**.) Activate a code. (☝ a code name in the Code System pane, ✔ **Activate**.) The text coded to that code in the active documents is displayed in the Retrieved Segments pane (see Fig 8.10). The contents can be saved or printed (e.g. ✔ **Project:Export:Retrieved Segments** menu). The text contents can be cut and pasted to your word processor.

121

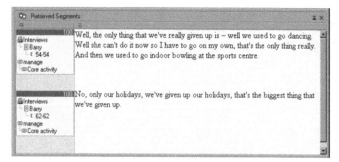

FIGURE 8.10   MAXqda Retrieved Segments pane

NVivo   Find the node you require and 🖱️ it. The text coded at the node is displayed with a new tab in the Detail View pane. The display includes headings indicating the documents the extracts come from and the number of times and how much of the document is coded. The contents can be cut and pasted to your word processor.

Key points

- CAQDAS can help considerably with the management of large, complex sets of data. However, the actual analytic ideas have to be provided by you, the researcher. Code and retrieve is a central function of most packages, but those examined in this chapter also have functions such as text and code searching that assist with the analysis too.
- Drawbacks reported by some users include feeling distant from the data and the software design being too influenced by grounded theory. However, modern packages have very good facilities for examining coding in context and going back to the original transcriptions, and although many were strongly influenced by grounded theory, they all now have a range of functions that tie them less closely to that approach.
- Three packages are featured: Atlas.ti, MAXqda and NVivo. All share the same basic facilities for handling online documents, coding, text retrieval, display of coding in context and memo writing.
- Before documents can be entered into the packages, they must be put into the correct format. The programs will accept files in rich text format (RTF) and this preserves fonts, size, paragraph layouts, colour, and so on.
- All the packages arrange things into projects (called hermeneutic units in Atlas.ti). The project contains all online documents, coding, memos,

attributes, charts, and so on. It is important to remember to create regular backups of your project.

- New documents can be introduced into a project and can then be inspected and printed.
- Each of the three programs allows the display of a code list, which can be arranged or displayed hierarchically. New codes can be added to this list and then passages of text can be identified that can be linked with these codes. Alternatively, new codes can be created directly by selecting passages of text and then naming the new code.
- Once coded, the text linked to a code can be retrieved into a single file or printout, or the coded passages can be viewed in context in the documents from which they come.

Further reading

These works provide more information about the use of computers and software in qualitative analysis:

Bazeley, P. (2007) *Qualitative Data Analysis with NVivo*. (2nd edn). London, Sage.

Fielding, N.G. and Lee, R.M. (1998) *Computer Analysis and Qualitative Research*. London: Sage.

Gibbs, G.R. (2002) *Qualitative Data Analysis: Explorations with NVivo*. Buckingham: Open University Press.

Lewins, A. and Silver, C. (2007) *Using Software in Qualitative Research: A Step-by-Step Guide*. London: Sage.

Seale, C.F. (2001) 'Computer-assisted analysis of qualitative interview data', in J.F. Gubrium and J.A. Holstein (eds). *Handbook of Interview Research: Context and Method*. Thousand Oaks, CA: Sage, pp. 651–70. See also the CAQDAS Networking Project at the University of Survey UK (caqdas.soc.surrey.ac.uk).

9
Searching and other analytic activities using software

Chapter objectives
After reading this chapter, you should

- see the relevance of searching as an important analytic technique and how computers excel at it;
- know more about two kinds of searching that are supported by CAQDAS and that are examined in this chapter: lexical searching and code searching;
- see that the former involves searching for text; and
- see that the latter enables you to make the kinds of analytic comparisons that were discussed in Chapter 6.

Searching

A lot of the time, doing qualitative analysis consists of reading the text and looking for things in the text. Sometimes this is difficult to do because it is hard to keep focused on the task. As you read the text it is easy to get interested in other things you come across – an occupational hazard of qualitative research, you might say. Also you can get bored and sloppy doing repetitive tasks like looking for the occurrences of specific terms or phrases. The risk is that this will produce biases in the way that you code and hence biases in the conclusions you might draw from the analysis. This is one area where computers can help. They do not suffer from boredom. Software searching for text, or a particular combination of coded text, will find every occurrence exactly as specified. Computer searching is no substitute for reading and thinking, but it can help with completeness and reliability both in examining the text and in the analysis.

Lexical searching

All three CAQDAS programs contain search tools that address these issues and allow you to search for text in a sophisticated way. Mostly, the use of text searching is for one of two reasons: to code text and to check for completeness. In Chapter 4 we saw how coding can be done by reading the documents and marking or coding sections of text. The process involves reading the text, deciding what it is about (its code or theme), linking it to a code (marking the text) and then looking for more passages on the same theme and coding them in the same way. There are several ways that searching can help with this.

Getting to know your data   Because you will still need to check the text you have found, this kind of searching can actually be used as a way of getting to know your data. A tactic you could adopt here is to search for terms that might be connected with your theoretical hunches and then inspect the passages retrieved or found in the original documents. The programs can create new coding as a result of the search. Bear in mind that you do not have to keep the results. At any time you can delete codes or uncode irrelevant passages or modify the text coded if the program has found too little or too much text.

Finding similar passages   A key activity in coding is looking for similar passages. Often passages already coded will contain terms, words or phrases that might occur elsewhere and indicate similar topic matter. Put these terms into the text search tool to find all the further occurrences. Clearly this does not mean that you have now found all the passages that can be coded with that code. There may be relevant passages that do not contain the words you have looked for or the respondents might be expressing themselves in other ways, using equivalent terms or synonyms of those you have searched for. Some of these you might pick up in the new passages found in the initial search operation, and these can then in turn be used as new search terms. Even so, there is no guarantee that the search will be complete. People may talk about the things you are interested in without mentioning any of the key terms you have searched for. You will still have to read the text and look for these other candidates for coding.

As well as failing to find some relevant passages, the computer search may find passages that are not relevant at all. These contain the search terms but are not in fact about the theme or idea in question. Sometimes this is because they are about the same subject but express a different or opposite view. In that case you might consider creating some new codes for them. In other cases there is no link at all with the original coding idea and the passages can be ignored (or uncoded). Thus each result of a search operation needs you, the human, to read through what is found and assess its meaning and relevance to the concepts you are working on. Using the software to search will ensure that you find things you might otherwise have missed, but it cannot ensure that you find only relevant text.

Looking for negative cases   Another important use for text searching is as a way of checking the completeness and validity of your coding. This often amounts to searching for what are known as negative cases, as discussed in Chapter 7 (see also Flick, 2007b). If, after exhaustive examination of the data, we can find only a few (or even better no) negative cases, then we can be more confident that our explanation has some validity and some grounding in the data. If you use text retrieved from a code to see if there are any negative cases pertaining to a specific context, you are relying on not having missed any significant examples when coding. Again the fallibility of the human researcher is a limitation. It is easy to miss key examples of text that should be coded at your developing code because you are not expecting to find it in this particular case or because it does not take the form of words you are thinking of. It is just these kinds of examples that are likely to constitute the negative cases that are so important in validity checking. Computers are not affected by such fallibilities. A computer search can therefore be a way of ensuring that there are no obvious examples of text (using terms and passages you know about or can think of) that should be coded to the code in question. However, useful though this is, it is important not to get carried away. The computer can never do all the work for you. There will always be examples of text that will not fit any text search pattern and will only be discovered by a careful reading of the documents.

This approach to searching is called lexical searching. It is a very useful approach not only for finding the occurrences of key terms, but also for examining the contexts in which they occur. This will enable you to discover the range of connotations of the terms and the kinds of imagery and metaphors associated with them. But, as Weaver and Atkinson (1994) point out, you need to be aware that the resultant coding may differ in significant ways from what you might produce using other strategies (e.g. close reading of the text). However, this can be an advantage. Other approaches tend to reflect, perhaps too much, the analyst's conceptions, whereas lexical searching is much more open-ended.

   When doing text searches, you do not have to keep exclusively to the terms and theme in question. Whilst checking through one passage of text you may well come across other ideas, themes or issues that are also worthy of coding. Quickly code the text at a new code and write a memo to capture the idea that you have had. Then move back to your original search.

To undertake a simple lexical search

 Atlas.ti

🗹 the Text Search button (🖳). The Text Search dialog opens (see Fig. 9.1).

FIGURE 9.1   The Atlas.ti Text Search dialog

Type in the term you want to search for and 🗹 **Case Sensitive** if you want that. 🗹 **Next**. The document text on display is searched and when a matching term is found the surrounding text is displayed with the term highlighted. The Text Search dialog is modeless, i.e. you can work on the document text while it remains open. Thus you can now code any appropriate text. 🗹 **Next**, to find the next occurrence. Once one document is completed you will be prompted whether you wish to search other documents in the hermeneutic unit (HU).

🖳 MAXqda

🗹 the Search button (🔍). The Search dialog opens. 🗹 **New** button and type in your search term or string. 🗹 the tick boxes to determine how you want to search (e.g. to find whole words only). 🗹 **Run Search** button. A Search Results window opens. (see Fig. 9.2). This shows which search strings were found in which documents. 🗹 them to show the string, selected in context, in the Text Browser pane. The Search Results window is modeless, i.e. you can work on the document text while it remains open. Thus you can now code any appropriate text you have found.

127

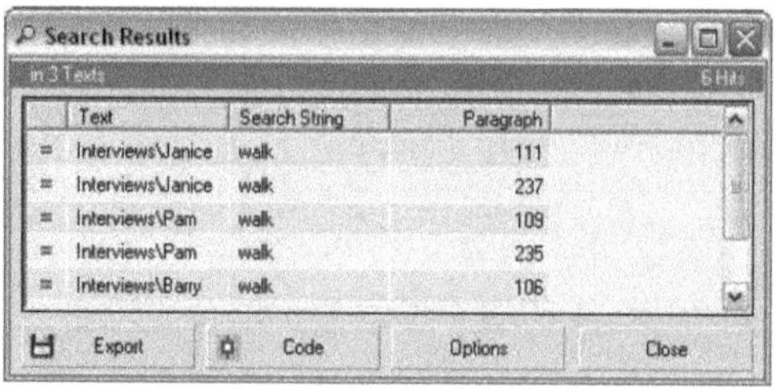

FIGURE 9.2   MAXqda Search Results window

![NVivo]

NVivo

🗸 **Queries** in the Navigation View pane list and 🗸 **Queries** folder that appears at the top of the pane. 🗸 **New** button (in the button bar). 🗸 **Text Search Query in this Folder ...** This opens the Text Search Query dialog (see Fig. 9.3).

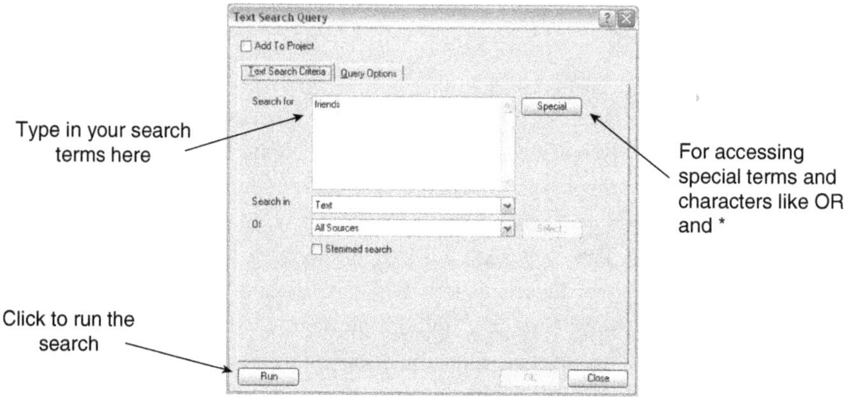

Type in your search terms here

For accessing special terms and characters like OR and *

Click to run the search

FIGURE 9.3   The NVivo Text Search Query dialog

Type in the search term or string, 🗸 Run. The results appear in the Detail View pane under a new tab. Each document in which some text was found is listed. 🗸 each to see the found text highlighted. (Scroll down to find further hits.) You can code any appropriate text as you read it.

You can search for more than one word at a time and for variations of the words by using wildcards and special characters. (To get the | character use the shift-\ key.)

128

	Search string	will find
Atlas.ti	walk|walking|walks	'walk' and/or 'walking' and/or 'walks', etc.
	walk*	any of 'walk', 'walking', 'walks', 'walked', 'walkers', etc.
MAXqda	Put in several words and click the **OR** radio button.	'walk' and/or 'walking' and/or 'walks', etc.
NVivo	walk OR walking OR walks walk*	'walk' and/or 'walking' and/or 'walks' any of 'walk', 'walking', 'walks', 'walked', 'walkers', etc.

An Example

To illustrate some of these processes, I will examine an example from a project that interviewed a large number of people in Yorkshire, UK who had been unemployed. Among other things, they were asked about their search for work. One activity that several respondents mentioned was the use of informal networks as a way of finding work, and one respondent mentioned the role of 'word of mouth' in finding out about vacancies. A text search on relevant words was undertaken to see if anyone else talked about this. For example, the words 'mate', 'relative' and 'friend' were searched for.

When you do a search like this, the text you find is a mixture of relevant material, relevant material with some bits missing, spurious finds, and appropriate finds but not relevant. The search above for 'mate', 'relative' and 'friend' gave the following text passages. (The words found are in bold so you can spot them. Also note that several of these speakers use Yorkshire dialect forms of speech such as omitting the definite article, ont' for 'on the' and 'I were' rather than 'I was'.)

TOM:

I usually looked in paper on a Wednesday or Thursday – local paper – that's all. Well, I tried to keep me ear to the ground, just in case anyone heard of anything. I kept asking **friend**s, asking around.

ASSAD:

I don't know ... I should say that word of mouth is more effective than anything. Maybe out of the blue a **mate** says 'I've got a decent job here you might fancy.' It beats anything else when you think about it.

129

BRIAN:

He's in chemical engineering at Stonehaven University, and I could work with him, but in fact, the number of places that are available are **relative**ly small, and if you're not an experienced lecturer, then of course the opportunities are less.

INT:

How did you come to hear about that job?

MALCOLM:

Friend of mine, lives just ont' road here. He's a manager in one of departments.

ANNA:

I did go back to work, September to March, before I were made redundant, and after that I were at home 12 month – well, 11 month – and I had a **friend** who worked in DHSS, and she told me, she says 'You want to get a note from your Doctor and say you're needed at home.'

The first two finds, extracts from Tom and Assad, and the fourth, from Malcolm, seem relevant. However, it is not clear whether Assad is actually using informal networks himself or just talking about them. So further checking with the rest of the transcript would be needed. The third find, from Brian, is spurious. It happened because the letters 'relative' were found at the start of the word 'relatively'. This can be avoided when searching by using an option to find whole words only or by inserting a space after the word in the search string. The last find, from Anna, is indeed about friends but it is not actually about using informal networks and is therefore not relevant. These examples illustrate how the text found by a text search needs checking through. You need to read it through and decide if the extract really is relevant or not. If the program has coded the text already (an option in Atlas.ti and NVivo), you will need to uncode the irrelevant finds and possibly extend the coding for others to include all relevant text. Otherwise you can simply ignore the false finds as you read them and in the case of the real 'hits' decide exactly what text you want to code with the new label.

Alongside getting hits that are not relevant, it is clear that a search based, say, just on the terms 'mates', 'friends' and 'relatives' will not find every discussion of using informal networks to find work. There are a couple of strategies you can adopt here to move forward:

- Look at the text you have found, as there may be other terms used that you can do further searches on that might find other relevant passages elsewhere. For example, on reading through all the related text found by the search using the terms 'friend', 'mate' and 'relative', the following additional words to search were identified: informal, in trade, in the trade, contacts, family. Although 'relative' was in the original search, it was also clear that in a few cases people referred directly to the particular relative, so searching for father, mother, daughter, son, uncle, aunt (at least) would also be useful.

- Keep a glossary of these terms and others you can add either by using a thesaurus or from your own knowledge. Search on these terms too and add any further relevant finds to the text coded to the original code. For example, looking up 'informal' in a thesaurus identified 'casual' and 'unofficial' as further terms that could be searched for. Keep this glossary and any strings you want to search for in a memo in your CAQDAS project as you can usually cut and paste them into the search dialog using the keyboard shortcuts, Ctrl-X and Ctrl-V. N.B. You can save combinations of words and text strings as queries or search settings (called swarms in Atlas./ti) to use again later. They can be reused on their own or, in Atlas.ti, as part of combinations with other strings and/or search swarms.

Searching for metaphors and accounts

So far I have treated text search as a way of creating and adding to the coding about thematic content, but you can also use text searching to examine the actual use of language, including the use of simile and metaphor. In other words, you might want to investigate the respondents' discourse. For example, you might look for evidence of fatalism in those looking for work. This might be done by searching for the specific use of words and phrases that express a fatalistic view. A quick read through one or two documents in the Job Search project produced the following terms that seem associated with fatalism: give up, pointless, in the trap, trapped, plodding on, can't handle any more, desperation, just luck, way it goes on the day. Use search to find all the occurrences of these words and terms.

In the case of metaphors and accounts (see Chapter 6), the text search tool can both alert you to the use of certain terms and give a good indication of how common the usage is. In looking for evidence for fatalistic discourse in the Unemployed in Yorkshire project, it became clear just how much respondents had talked about 'luck'. After searching for the string 'luck|lucky|unlucky' and reading the paragraphs in which the terms occurred, I could see that respondents were mainly trying to account for why they remained unemployed or how others managed to get jobs. Note that this is just the start of an investigation of account giving by unemployed people. It is necessary to check what other kind of accounts people were giving. Again, some reading is required, but this can be complemented by searching when some new terms are discovered. For example, some respondents used the term 'fortunate' in their speeches, picked up by the search for 'luck'. This could be added to the search string.

Searching is good for looking for thematic items where the words used indicated the thematic content, but it is not so good for narrative use. Here, what is important is not what it being said but rather how it is said, why it is said and what the person intends by saying it. So a simple search for words (even using a glossary) will not suffice. However, here you can construct a different kind of search. For example, you can look for the kind of words people use when making narrative moves. For instance, when engaging in some kinds of talk, respondents may announce that they are about to appeal to a certain aspect of their identity by using terms like 'speaking as a fireman ... ', 'in my experience as a grandmother ... ' or 'what all us cyclists agree on is ... '. You could search for the terms 'speaking as', 'in my experience as' and 'all ... agree on' and other similar ones to find these narrative moves. To summarize, Box 9.1 suggests some good practice when searching.

Box 9.1   Using the text search facility creatively and to enhance validity

- Use searching and then reading the finds to become familiar with the data.
- Search using further relevant words and terms in the passages that you have examined.
- Merge the results of new searches with relevant previous codes created from searches.
- Construct a glossary of terms to search for. Add to these using a thesaurus or your own knowledge. Keep the glossary in a memo.
- Look for use of certain types of language such as use of metaphor and investigate contrasts between different subsets of the project data such as young and old respondents.
- Use searching to look for negative cases, those that do not fit your assumed explanation.
- Check by searching to see if a theme you think is dominant really is. It may occur less often than you imagined.
- Use searching to try and achieve completeness in your coding, to ensure that all occurrences of the theme have actually been coded.
- Spread finds to paragraphs (in NVivo and MAXqda and autocoding in Atlas.ti) and review finds, adding to and subtracting from the coded text as appropriate.
- Use search on your memos to help keep control of your analysis.

Adapted from Gibbs (2002, p. 123).

Attributes

Attributes are a form of variable data used in qualitative analysis. Typically each case in a study might be assigned a value for each attribute. (They may have no value if the attribute is not applicable.) Common examples are the gender of a respondent (male or female), age of respondent in years and place of residence. Often this information is recorded in the document summary sheet. This is similar to the use of categorical variables in quantitative research, but in qualitative analysis we can also apply attributes and values to other units in a study, like settings or events. Thus for settings, like different companies or corporations in a study, we might record the number of staff, company name and manager, or for events, the date, time and place. Such attributes are usually matters of fact about the person, setting, and so on, however, later in your analysis you might develop classifications or even a taxonomy that can be represented as an attribute and applied, perhaps, to different cases. Most commonly, attributes are used to control retrievals and searches using codes so that you can make comparisons (see the next section).

To set up attributes in a project

Atlas.ti

The program does not handle attributes directly, but you can collect documents and codes into families and use these in searching. **✔ Documents:Edit Families:Open Family Manager**. The Primary Document Family manager opens (see Fig. 9.4). To create a new family **✔** on the New Family button (⊜) or **✔ Families:New Family**. Type in a name for the family (effectively an attribute value), **✔ OK**. To assign documents to this family, **✔** a non-member document (on the right) and **✔** < button.

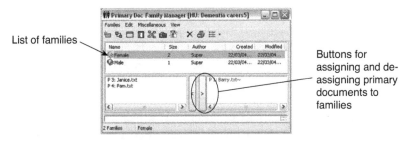

List of families

Buttons for assigning and de-assigning primary documents to families

FIGURE 9.4   Atlas.ti Primary Document Family Manager

Codes and memos can also be assigned to families in the same fashion using the Code families and Memo families managers.

MAXqda   **✔** the Attributes button (▥). The Attributes dialog opens. (see Fig. 9.5). **◨** any of the column titles (e.g. Textgroup), **✔ Insert New Attributive**. In the dialog, give the attribute a name, e.g. Gender, and choose an appropriate type for it. (If the values will be just text, then choose **String**.) **✔ OK**.   **133**

A new column appears, headed with your variable name. a cell in this column to type in a value for this document. After you have entered a few values you can use the pull-down menu to select a pre-entered value. a cell then the triangle at the right-hand end to get a pull-down menu. the value you want (see Fig. 9.5).

	Textgroup	Textname	Creation Date	Number of Coded Segments	Number of Memos	Author	Bytes	Gender
	Interviews	Barry	14/03/2004 16:16	16	2		25694	Male
	Interviews	Pam	14/03/2004 16:20	9	0		25779	Female
	Interviews	Janice	14/03/2004 16:20	0	0		25908	Female

Pull-down menu of pre-entered attribute values

FIGURE 9.5   MAXqda Table of Attributes

NVivo

To create a new attribute, **Classifications** in the Navigation View pane list and **Attributes** folder that appears at the top of the pane. **New** button (in the button bar) **Attribute in This Folder ...** This opens the New Attribute dialog. Type in the new attribute name. **Values** tab, **Add**. Type in the first of the values you need. **Add** to add as many more values as you need. **OK**.

In NVivo only cases or nodes may have attributes. So first you may need to assign your documents to cases. For example, if each interview is stored as one document, then each document can be a case. **Sources** in the Navigation View pane list and **Documents** folder that appears at the top of the pane. If each document displayed is to be made a case, then select all the documents (CTRL-A). Then on the selected documents, **Create as: Create Cases**. In the Select Location dialog that appears, **Folders** and then **Cases** that appears in the Name list on the right. **OK**. Cases with the same names as the documents are now automatically created.

To assign attribute values to these cases, **Nodes** in the Navigation View pane list and **Cases** folder that appears near the top of the pane. The list of cases appears in the List View pane. on a case. **Case Properties**. The Case Properties dialog opens. **Attribute Values** tab. Choose a value for this case from the pop-down menus of values against each relevant attribute you have created. **Apply** (see Fig. 9.6). **OK**. Repeat for all the other cases.

134

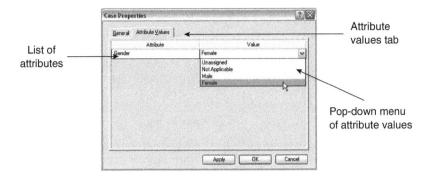

FIGURE 9.6   NVivo Case Properties dialog

Searching with codes and attributes

All three programs contain functions for searching and retrieving text that has already been coded – searching with codes and/or attributes. This allows a very rich set of comparisons to be made. All the different kinds of comparisons discussed in Chapter 6 can be carried out using the Search or Query tool and retrieving and inspecting the coded text.

When doing text search it is clear that what is being searched for is text and what is being searched in is text. This is less obvious when searching with codes and/or attributes, but it is important to recognize that the same is true. In these cases, what is compared in the search is the actual text coded at or linked to the code or attribute. Thus in the simplest case, if you search for one code *or* another, what is compared is the text coded with these codes. The search will find all the text coded at either code, if any (including that coded at both codes, if any).

All three programs allow two or more codes (and sometimes attributes too) to be searched for in combination. Such combination is divided into two kinds, Boolean and proximity. Boolean searches combine codes using the logical terms like 'and', 'or' and 'not'. This type of search is named after the mathematician, Boole, who first formalized them. Common Boolean searches are 'or' (also referred to as 'combination' or 'union') and 'and' (also called 'intersection'). Proximity searches rely on the coded text being near, after or perhaps overlapping some other coded text. Commonly used proximity searches are 'followed by' (also referred to as 'sequence' or 'preceding') and 'near' (also referred to as 'co-occurrence'). Table 9.1 explains how they work and gives some examples. Although both Boolean and proximity searches are useful for investigating the data and checking hunches, the Boolean searches are most useful in examining hypotheses or ideas about the data and rely on consistent and accurate coding, whereas proximity searches can be used more speculatively and to explore the data, often at an early stage of coding.

135

TABLE 9.1 Common Boolean and proximity searches using code A and code B

Search	Will find	Common use
A and B	Only the text that is coded with both A and B and not any text that is coded with only one of the codes A or B or neither.	If A is 'gives account' and B is 'plays truant', then A **and** B will find all the places the respondent explains why they stay away from school.
A or B	Any text that is coded with A or B or both. N.B. It is often useful to do an 'or' search on three or more codes at once. This will find text coded with any of the codes.	In a project on people who have separated from their partners, if A is 'abandoned', B is 'drifted apart' and C is 'mutual agreement', then A **or** B **or** C will find and bring together all the ways the people describe their reasons for separation.
A followed by B	The text that is coded with code A where it is followed by some text coded with code B. You may have to specify how closely it is followed.	In the same project on people who have separated from their partners, if A is 'turning point' and B is 'training', then A followed by B (retrieving B) will show where people talk about training they have had after their turning point.
A near B	Only the text that is coded with one code that appears near text coded with the other (before or after or even overlapping). You will need to define what near means, for example 'within 2 paragraphs'.	In the homelessness project, if A is 'becoming homeless' and B is 'anger', then A near B (retrieving A) will show where people talk about becoming homeless that is associated with their expressing anger.

For example, to produce output that would enable you to assemble the contents for each of the cells in Table 6.5 in Chapter 6, you would need text coded using codes for 'Routine', 'Haphazard' and 'Entrepreneurial' and either an attribute for Gender or document families for 'male' and 'female'. Then you could do a search for text with the attribute value 'male' **and** coded with the code 'Routine', and then text with value 'female' **and** coded with the code 'Routine'. Then repeat this for 'Haphazard' and 'Entrepreneurial'.

Searching for text coded 'Routine' AND with an attribute value of either 'male' or 'female'

Atlas.ti   Set up a family of male documents and one for female documents (as above). ✔ the Query tool icon in the icon

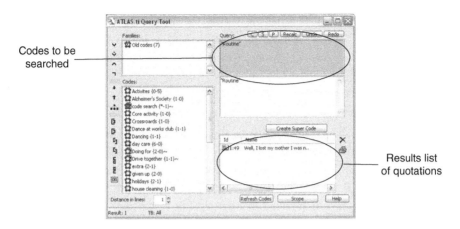

Codes to be
searched

Results list
of quotations

FIGURE 9.7   The Atlas.ti Query Tool dialog

bar (⊞), the Atlas.ti Query Tool dialog opens (see Fig. 9.7).
✔ the code 'Routine' in the **Codes:** list. Its name is
copied to the **Query:** list. A list of the quotations found is
displayed in the result list (bottom right). ✔ the sample
text for each quotation in the result list to see the coded
text highlighted in its document displayed in the Primary
Document Area.

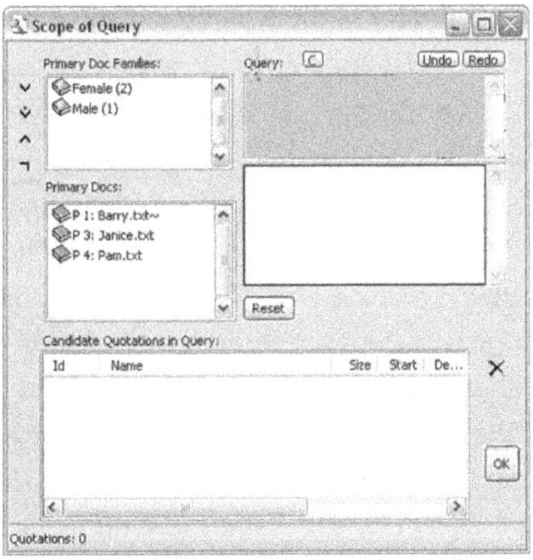

FIGURE 9.8   Atlas.ti Scope of Query dialog

✔ **Scope** button. The Scope of Query dialog opens (see
Fig. 9.8). ✔ the clear button (**C**) to clear any previous selections.
✔ the family 'Male' in the **Primary Doc Families:** list. The
family 'Male' is copied to the **Query:** list. Also the list of quotations showing in the Result list of the Query Tool is reduced   **137**

to show only those quotations in documents in the male 'family'. ✔ **OK**. Inspect the quotations in the Primary Document area by clicking on each in turn. Repeat this process but ✔ the family 'Female' in the Scope of Query dialog to show only those quotations in documents in the female 'family'.

 MAXqda

First you need to activate just the male texts. ➔ **Text Groups** in the Document System pane, ✔ **Activation by Attributes**. ✔ **New**, put a tick in the Gender box (or whatever you have called the attribute), ✔ **OK**. Select 'Male' from the pop-down menu on the **Value** box, ✔ **Activate** (assuming you have already assigned your documents to the attribute value 'Male' or 'Female'). In the Code System pane, find and ➔ the code 'Routine', ✔ **Activate**. The Retrieved Segments pane will now show those segments of text that are coded with 'Routine' in the male documents only. For the female texts, ➔ **Text Groups** in the Document System pane, ✔ **Activation by Attributes**. Select 'Female' from the pop-down menu on the **Value** box, ✔ **Activate**. Assuming that the code 'Routine' is still activated, those segments of text that are coded with 'Routine' in the female documents will now be displayed in the Retrieved segments pane.

NVivo

✔ **Queries** in the Navigation View pane list and ✔ **Queries** folder that appears at the top of the pane. ✔ **New** button (in the button bar), ✔ **Coding Query in this Folder ...** This opens the Coding Query dialog (see Fig. 9.9). ✔ the **Advanced** tab. Select **Coded by** and **Selected Node** from the pop-down menus near the bottom of the dialog. ✔ **Select ...** and from the Select Project Item dialog that opens, select the node 'Routine'. ✔ **OK**. ✔ **Add to List**. The first search criterion is added to the criteria panel above (see Fig. 9.9). Select **Attribute Condition** from the pop-down menus near the bottom of the dialog. ✔ **Select ...** and from the Coding Search Item dialog that opens, select the attribute 'Gender', 'equals value' and 'Male'. ✔ **OK**. ✔ **Add to List**. This criterion is added to the list with, by default, 'AND'. ✔ **Run**. A new tab in the Detail View pane is opened, showing the text found by the search. This shows text coded by 'Routine' in the male cases. Repeat the search but with attribute Gender value =

female. Flip between the two tabs showing the results to examine the differences.

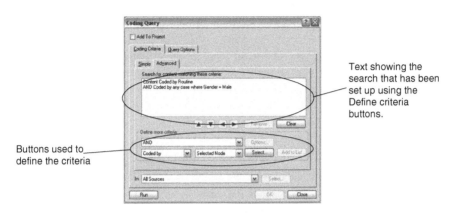

Text showing the search that has been set up using the Define criteria buttons.

Buttons used to define the criteria

FIGURE 9.9   NVivo Coding Query dialog

There is a lot more to searching than just searching for text and/or codes. All three programs allow quite complex searches and complex combinations of codes (and families in Atlas.ti and attributes for NVivo and MAXqda). One particularly powerful form of search is the ability of NVivo to do what are called matrix searches. With these you can produce, in a single search, text finds that support some of the tables I described in Chapter 6. The idea of a matrix search is that you search one group of codes against another group of codes (or in the case of NVivo, group of codes or attributes). Using NVivo in the example from Chapter 6 will enable you to find in one go the six groups of text obtained from searching gender (male or female) against the three codes, 'Routine', 'Haphazard' and 'Entrepreneurial'. The type of search you choose to do ('and' in the example above) is applied to each pair of codes and/or attributes in turn: 'male' with 'Routine', 'female' with 'Routine', 'male' with 'Haphazard', 'female' with 'Haphazard', 'male' with 'Entrepreneurial' and 'female' with 'Entrepreneurial'.

Pros and cons of searching

Searching is one of the most powerful tools available in CAQDAS programs. It can be used for both an exploratory approach to the data, just to see what is there, and for checking hunches. Text search, as I have described above, is very good for exploration, but you can use code searching in this way too. For example it can be used to elaborate the dimensions of responses and you might use it as a way of developing a taxonomy and improving the content and structure of your code hierarchy. For example, in the Unemployed in Yorkshire project, imagine you have done a code search to bring together all the text about the evaluation of various work-finding services (e.g. an 'or' search). Reading through this text you might note that there are several different kinds of response to the services. Some respondents found them helpful, others found them inaccessible, others found them irrelevant to their needs. You can create new codes for these ideas (code to them from the text you have found) as a dimension of the concept of evaluation.

Searching for codes can also be used for checking hunches and ideas – in fact, a form of hypothesis checking. For example, in the study of carers for those with dementia, you might have a hunch that men who are carers get more or different kinds of assistance from both state services and from voluntary and charitable organizations. A search of the attribute/family gender against the codes for the various kinds of help given by the various services and organizations will retrieve text for men and for women that can be compared. You might find that some codes are entirely absent for women, indicating that they did not mention this kind of help at all. But more important than the absence or presence of coded text is a comparison of the actual content of what men said about the services and what women said. By making such comparisons you will get a real feel for how the assistance women and men get is different (or similar).

Reliability and searching

On the other hand, code and attribute searching is only as good as your coding or assignment of attributes. If your codes are poorly defined, inconsistently applied and even conceptually overlapping and confused, then the results of code searches will be biased and unreliable. It is up to you to ensure that codes are clearly defined and that the text coded at them is relevant and consistent. You will need to keep a constant eye out for text that has been missed in your coding. But even with near-perfect coding, code and attribute searching is not a perfect tool for hypothesis testing and pattern searching. Finding relationships (or failing to find them) is only reliable if the text reflects the assumptions built into such searching. These assumptions include that the recorded text is complete (it records all the relevant things that actually happened, could have been said, etc.) and the text is well structured (all the discussion about an issue is near together in the documents).

The last point is a particular problem for proximity searches. These rely on the fact that when people talk about one thing, they tend to talk about related things just before or just afterwards. This may not be the case. For instance:

- People may draw together particular issues at one moment because it serves their purpose at that point in the interview or discussion, and later they may bring together quite different sets of related issues.
- Not uncommonly, later in an interview respondents remember things they meant to say earlier.

For this reason, related issues may not appear together or even near each other in transcripts. It is therefore worth remembering the caution expressed by Coffey and Atkinson:

> Given the inherently unpredictable structure of qualitative data, co-occurrence or proximity does not necessarily imply an analytically significant relationship among categories. It is as shaky an assumption as one that assumes greater significance of commonly occurring codes. Analytic significance is not guaranteed by frequency, nor is a relationship guaranteed by proximity. Nevertheless, a general heuristic value may be found for such methods for checking out ideas and data, as part of the constant interplay between the two as the research process unfolds. (Coffey and Atkinson, 1996, p. 181)

Key Points

- Searching for text (lexical searching using a computer) can help analysis by finding similar passages for coding, looking for negative cases or simply letting you become familiar with your data. Such searching is efficient; all occurrences of the search terms will be found whether they are relevant or not. Consequently, the results of searching have to be checked to make sure they are relevant.
- A lexical search is only as good as the terms searched for, so compiling a list of related terms to be searched for is necessary. These can be provided by existing understanding and theory, by using a thesaurus, or by inspecting text near the found terms for related words.
- Attributes are a simple way of storing straightforward information about cases and settings. They can be used to refine searches.
- All three packages also support searching using codes. In this case, what is searched for is any text that matches the specified code(s). Such searches can be combined in Boolean (e.g. A and B, A or B) and proximity (e.g. A followed by B, A near B) searches.
- Both lexical and code searches can be used to explore and become familiar with your data. Searching for codes can also be used to look for patterns (using comparisons) and for checking hunches about relationships in the data.

Further reading

These books explore the use of computers in analyzing qualitative data in more detail:

Gibbs, G.R. (2002) *Qualitative Data Analysis: Explorations with NVivo.* Buckingham: Open University Press.

Miles, M.B. and Huberman, A.M. (1994) *Qualitative Data Analysis: A Sourcebook of New Methods.* Beverly Hills, CA: Sage.

Ritchie, J. and Lewis, J. (eds) (2003) *Qualitative Research Practice: A Guide for Social Science Students and Researchers.* London: Sage.

10
Putting it all together

Chapter objectives
After reading this chapter, you should

- see the different steps of qualitative analysis that this book was about in context and relation to each other;
- take up a more comprehensive perspective on qualitative analysis, again putting coding in the context of reading and writing; and
- know more about issues of analytic quality.

Reading

One of the things found most difficult by those who are new to qualitative analysis is making a full interpretation of their data. Novice analysts read their transcripts and tend to take the immediate, impressionistic, surface reading – the interpretation of the content that comes first to their attention. Such an interpretation fails to recognize that qualitative data are multi-layered and may be interpreted in different, but equally plausible, ways.

This book has tried to indicate some of the techniques or approaches that will help you find interpretations and move them from the descriptive to more analytic levels. A key example of this is to read the text (or examine the non-textual data) more carefully – to undertake what I have called intensive reading. There are always lots of things going on in a text or in a setting. Not only is the content of what is being said rich and diverse – people are doing things that can be understood in several ways at once – but people are indicating things about themselves and their world by their actions and the way they express themselves. Read and reread the text (or re-examine the non-textual data) so that you become thoroughly familiar with it and each time you do so ask new questions of it.

Writing

All qualitative analysis involves writing. Having gone to all the trouble of collecting data and analyzing it and, of course, given the effort put in by participants in providing you with data, it makes a lot of sense to write up the results and publish them. But writing in qualitative data analysis is more than that. Writing about your data and even rewriting it are essential aspects of the analysis itself. Writing about the data is both a form of record-keeping and also a creative process in which you develop ideas about your project. A principal form of this is writing notes and memos. All this will help you to generate ideas that can form part of your analysis. It will provide evidence of that process and identify the way that your own position, your perspective, theories and even biases, might have shaped or created the analysis you have come up with. Writing about the process of analysis, perhaps by keeping a research diary, will help you become reflexive about your work and make you aware of how your own position and your interests and biases have guided your analysis.

Coding

In this book I have given a central place to coding. Not all qualitative researchers code, but for most it is a key technique for sorting out their data and keeping on top of its sheer volume. Coding can be used in a variety of ways. The most common is the categorization of the thematic content of your data. This facilitates the relatively rapid retrieval and comparison of all the data marked with the same code that are examples of some action, setting, strategy, meaning, emotion, and so on that you are interested in. But coding can be used more idiosyncratically along with other ways of marking the text – highlighting, circling, underlining, commenting – just to indicate matters of interest to you, perhaps to be returned to later in the analysis. Used in this way, coding is more akin to bookmarking than categorizing. Line-by-line coding tends to be like this, but you will probably find much of the material you have coded line by line or otherwise marked can eventually be categorized with more systematic, thematic codes.

Codes represent some concept, theme or idea in your analysis and you should keep a codebook that lists all your codes along with their definitions and memos about them. Some analysts suggest that simply listing your codes in this way is not analysis; it is just a way of organizing it. Others argue that this organization can have some analytic purpose and thus is a key part of the analysis. The point is that your write-up should never rely just on the main codes from your codebook. There are many examples of poor student work – and published work – that tend to the impressionistic and anecdotal and are simply organized as a description or summary of each of the main themes found in the data. Whilst this can be interesting, especially if the study is about a setting or situation that others have rarely experienced, often it just summarizes what we already know. You need to go beyond this. Re-examine the data and find phenomena that are not necessarily immediately obvious from what is being said or done. Excellent analytic work does this and also brings to bear theory to explain and understand what is happening. Outstanding work might even suggest new theory or at least new applications of existing theory.

Relationships and patterns

One way to go beyond the descriptive and impressionistic is to look for patterns and relationships in your data. Look for differences and similarities across different cases, settings, actors, situations, motives, and so on and use attributes/variables and tables to investigate them. One consequence of such searches is that you are faced with the question of why the differences and similarities you have found occur, and you are obliged to offer explanations and reasons for the patterns. The richness of qualitative data is helpful here. Thick description provides evidence of people's motives, intentions and strategies and therefore can offer suggestions as to their reasons for doing things (even if they are not aware of them at that moment and not telling you about them directly). But there is a danger of offering explanations on the basis of partial or biased data. That is why it is important to be exhaustive and analytic in the examination of your data. You need to be open about the degree to which your explanations are based on common situations or unusual ones and the extent to which your evidence gives you confidence in your explanations.

Analytic quality

There is no simple formula you can follow to ensure that your analysis is of good quality (see also Flick, 2007b, for a more extended discussion) and that it does not descend, without your realizing it, into anecdotalism, bias and partiality. The only advice here is to do your analysis carefully and comprehensively. By the use of code hierarchies, tables, constant comparison and, of course, by frequent rereading of your transcripts, notes and memos you can make sure that your analysis is not only exhaustive but is well balanced and well supported by the data you have collected. CAQDAS programs can help ensure comprehensive and exhaustive studies, but they are not vital, even though many researchers now find them an invaluable support for their analytic activities. Computers cannot do the interpreting for you. In the end, it is your responsibility, the human researcher, to come up with interpretations, to develop analytical explanations and to underpin your overall analysis by appropriate theory. Doing this assiduously, comprehensively and exhaustively will help ensure that your analysis is not only of good quality, but ultimately that it is interesting, persuasive and significant.

‖ Glossary

Accounts A specific form of narrative in which respondents try to account for, justify, excuse, legitimate, etc., their actions or situation.

Anonymization The process in both transcriptions and research reports of changing names, places, details, etc., that might identify people and organizations so that they cannot be identified and yet the overall meaning is preserved.

Attributes General properties possessed by one or more persons, cases or settings. Very like a variable in quantitative analysis. Similarities within or differences between groups can be identified using attributes. An attribute (e.g. gender) may have several values (e.g. male, female, not relevant) and any particular case may be assigned just one value for each attribute.

Auto-coding The function in some CAQDAS programs to code the results of a search.

Axial coding In grounded theory, the second stage of coding in which the relationships of categories are explored and connections between them are made. The analyst begins to select codes that represent and highlight the core issues or themes in the data.

Bias Any influence that systematically distorts the results of a research study. In a realist approach this will obscure the true nature of what is being studied, and may be caused by the researcher or by the procedures for collecting data, including sampling. From a relativist or interpretive perspective it makes little sense as there is no true nature about which the findings may be biased, although a reflexive account of the research does address the issues of trust that the concept of bias addresses.

Biography An extended, written account or narrative of a person's life. It usually has a structure and is expressed in key themes, often with an **epiphany** or turning point. The narrative is usually chronological.

CAQDAS Computer-assisted qualitative data analysis. N.B Computers only assist. The software does not analyze. Term introduced by Fielding and Lee (1991).

Case   An individual unit being studied. A case can be a person, an institution, an event, a country or region, a family, a setting or an organization. Which is used depends on the particular study being undertaken.

Code   A term that represents an idea, theme, theory, dimension, characteristic, etc., of the data. Passages of text, images, etc., in a qualitative analysis study can be linked to the same code to show that they represent the same idea, theme, characteristic, etc.

Codebook   A list of the codes in use in a qualitative data analysis project, usually containing their definitions and a set of rules or guidelines for coding. Also called a coding frame.

Coding   The action of identifying a passage of text in a document or an image or part of an image that exemplifies some idea or concept and then connecting it to a named code that represents that idea or concept. This shows that it shares the characteristics indicated by the code and/or its definition with other similarly coded passages or texts. All the passages and images associated with a code can be examined together and patterns identified.

Coding stripes   Traditionally these are (coloured) stripes drawn down the margin of a text with an associated name to show how lines have been coded. In software this is shown by vertical coloured lines displayed (optionally) in a pane to the side of a document (on the left in MAXqda and on the right in Atlas.ti and NVivo). Each is named with the title of the code at which the text is coded.

Comparative analysis   Analysis where data from different settings or groups at the same point in time or from the same settings or groups over a period of time are analyzed to identify similarities and differences. (See also **Constant comparison.**)

Confidentiality   Systematic protection of the nature of information supplied by respondents so that it is not disclosed to parties other than the research team.

Constant comparison   A procedure used during **grounded theory** research whereby newly gathered data are continually compared with previously collected data and their coding in order to refine the development of theoretical categories. The purpose is to test emerging ideas that might take the research in new and fruitful directions.

Data   Items or units of information generated and recorded through social research (singular = datum). Data can be numerical (quantitative) or consist of words, images or objects (qualitative). Naturally occurring data are those that record events that would have occurred whether a researcher was present or not. Nevertheless, data are not 'out there' waiting to be collected. Data are the product of the research itself and are determined by the research process.

Data archives A form of archive that contains data generated by research studies. These are commonly quantitatively coded material from surveys, or qualitative material collected as part of social research studies, and they have been made available through the archive for secondary analysis.

Descriptive coding Coding to codes that simply refers to surface features of the people, events, settings, etc., in a study.

Epiphany An episode in someone's biography or life history that is a turning point. It separates the **biography** into contrasted periods, before and after the epiphany. People commonly describe themselves as having been changed by the epiphany or being a different person after it.

Ethics A branch of philosophy and a field of everyday thinking that deals with questions of what is morally right and wrong.

Ethnography A multi-method qualitative approach that examines specific social settings and systematically describes the culture of a group of people. The goal of ethnographic research is to understand the natives'/ insiders' view of their own world. Originally associated with anthropology and still favours naturalistic forms of data collection such as fieldwork, that is, time spent 'living' with a community.

Field notes These are notes taken by the researcher about their thoughts and observations when they are in the field 'environment' they are researching.

Generalizability The degree to which it is justifiable to apply to a wider population explanations and descriptions that research has found apply in a particular sample or example.

Grounded theory An inductive form of qualitative research, introduced by Glaser and Strauss, where data collection and analysis are conducted together. Constant comparison and theoretical sampling are used to support the systematic discovery of theory from the data. Thus theories remain grounded in the observations rather than generated in the abstract. Sampling of cases, settings or respondents is guided by the need to test the limits of developing explanations, which are constantly grounded in the data being analyzed.

Idealism The view that the world exists in people's minds and there is no simple external reality independent of people's thoughts.

Induction The logical move from a number of specific statements, events or observations to a general theory or explanation of the situation or phenomenon.

Informed consent The process of obtaining the voluntary agreement of individuals to participate in research that is based on their full understanding of the possible benefits and risks to themselves.

Interpretive coding   The coding of data in which the researcher interprets the contents to generate some concept, idea, explanation or understanding. Interpretation may be based on respondents' own views and experiences, the researcher's view or understanding, or on some pre-existing theory or framework.

Intertextuality   The echo of one text in another text. This may take the form of explicit cross-references or stylistic approach or implicit themes.

Lexical searching   Text searching that is concerned to find the occurrence of words and phrases used by respondents and investigate their context of use.

Life history   An interview form in which the focus is the life story of the participant. Such interviews tend to be structured around the chronology of the life course, but are otherwise relatively open-ended.

Memo   A document used in analysis containing the researcher's commentary on the primary data or codes of the project. Memos may be separate documents, linked to particular data (especially in a CAQDAS program) or collected to form a research diary.

Metaphor   The use of imagery in speech or text as a kind of rhetorical device. Metaphor use may indicate culturally shared ideas or difficulties in expression.

Model   A mapping device, often expressed in a chart or diagram, designed to represent the relationship between key elements in a field of study. Models may be predictive, causal or descriptive, and may be discursive, mathematical or graphical.

Narrative   Text or speech that tells a story of events and experiences, usually involving the personal dimension and told from the individual's point of view.

Narrative analysis   Form of discourse analysis that seeks to study the textual devices at work in the constructions of process or sequence within a text.

Open coding   The first stage of coding in **grounded theory**, where text is read reflectively to identify relevant categories. New codes are created as the text is read and are given a theoretical or analytic (and not merely descriptive) name. Relevant text is coded together at the same code. The analyst may try to develop dimensions for the categories (codes).

Participant observation   The method most commonly adopted by ethnographers, whereby the researcher participates in the life of a community or group, while making observations of members' behaviour. This may be covert or overt.

Postmodernism   A social movement or fashion amongst intellectuals that rejects modernist values of rationality, progress and a conception of social science as a search for overarching explanations of human nature or the social and cultural world. Instead, postmodernists celebrate the fall of such oppressive grand narratives, emphasizing the fragmented and dispersed nature of contemporary experience. In its extreme form it rejects the presence of absolute truths or knowledge, and the ability of science to explain social phenomena.

Realism   The view that a reality exists independent of our thoughts and beliefs or even our existence. Research can give us direct information about this reality rather than just constructions of it. However, some more subtle realists do recognize constructive properties in language.

Reflexivity   In a broad sense this refers to the view that researchers inevitably, in some way or another, reflect the views and interests of their milieu. It also refers to the capacity of researchers to reflect upon their actions and values during research, whether in producing data or writing accounts.

Relativism   In a conceptual or ethical sense, the rejection of absolute standards for judging truth or morality. Cultural relativism is the view that different cultures define phenomena in different ways, so that the perspective of one cannot be used to judge or even understand that of another.

Reliability   The degree to which different observers, researchers, etc. (or the same observers, etc., on different occasions) make the same observations or collect the same data about the same object of study. The concept is highly contentious in qualitative research where it is often not clear what the same object of study is.

Research ethics   A set of standards and principles about what is acceptable or right and what is wrong or unacceptable when conducting social research.

Retrieving codes   The process of collecting together all the text that has been coded at a single code in order to examine it for patterns and commonalities.

Rhetoric   The use of language to persuade or influence people and the study of such methods. It involves linguistic strategies used by speakers or authors of texts to convey particular impressions or reinforce specific interpretations.

Saturation   In grounded theory, the situation where predictions and expectations based on existing data and categories are repeatedly confirmed by data from additional categories or cases. The additional categories or cases seem to contain no new ideas and they are then said to be saturated. The search for further appropriate instances seems futile and data collection can cease. Also referred to as data saturation.

Search   One of the core functions of CAQDAS; it includes both lexical searching (searching for words and phrases repeatedly in text) and code searching. In the case of code searching, what is found by the search are passages of text that are coded (or not) in specified ways and that are related to other coded passages in specified ways (e.g. they overlap, they are coded by both codes).

Selective coding   The final stage of **grounded theory** in which a central phenomenon or core category is identified and all other categories are related to it.

Social constructionism   The epistemological view that the phenomena of the social and cultural world and their meanings are not objective but are created in human social interaction, that is, they are socially constructed. The approach often, though not exclusively, draws on idealist philosophy.

Taxonomy   A strict hierarchical classification of items where the relationship between parent and child items is that of 'is a kind of ... ' or 'is a type of ... '.

Text   In the narrow sense, this means a written document. However, the usage has been extended to refer to anything that can be 'read', that is, has a meaning that can be interpreted. Examples include advertisements, pieces of music or films. Semioticians have considered items as diverse as wrestling matches and Coca Cola cans as 'texts', worthy of analysis for their cultural connotations.

Themes   A recurring issue or an idea or concept either derived from prior theory or from respondents' lived experience that emerges during the analysis of qualitative data. It can be used to establish a code with which text can be coded.

Transcription   The process of transferring audio or video recordings of speech or handwritten notes into a typed or word-processed form. In some cases, special characters may be used to indicate aspects of how words were spoken.

Validity   The extent to which an account accurately represents the social phenomenon to which it refers. In realist research it refers to the degree to which the research provides a true picture of the situation and/or people being studied and is often referred to as internal validity. External validity refers to the extent to which the data collected from the group or situation studied can be generalized to a wider population. Postmodernists, who contest that research can ever provide a single true picture of the world, contest the very possibility of validity.

▌▌ References

Angrosino, M. (2007) *Doing Ethnographic and Observational Research*. (Book 3 of *The SAGE Qualitative Research Kit*) London: Sage.

Arksey, H. and Knight, P. (1999) *Interviewing for Social Scientists*. London: Sage.

Atkinson, J.M. and Heritage, J. (eds) (1984) *Structures of Social Action: Studies in Conversation Analysis*. Cambridge: Cambridge University Press.

Banks, M. (2007) *Using Visual Data in Qualitative Research* (Book 5 of *The SAGE Qualitative Research Kit*) London: Sage.

Barbour, R. (2007) *Doing Focus Groups* (Book 4 of *The SAGE Qualitative Research Kit*). London: Sage.

Bazeley, P. (2007) *Qualitative Data Analysis with NVivo*. (2nd edn). London: Sage.

Becker, H.S. (1986) *Writing for Social Scientists: How to Start and Finish Your Thesis, Book or Article*. Chicago: University of Chicago Press.

Bird, C.M. (2005) 'How I stopped dreading and learned to love transcription', *Qualitative Inquiry*, 11(2): 226–48.

Bogdan, R. and Biklen, S.K. (1992) *Qualitative Research for Education: An Introduction to Theory and Methods*. Boston: Allyn & Bacon.

Brewer, J.D. (2000) *Ethnography*. Buckingham: Open University Press.

Bryman, A. (1988) *Quantity and Quality in Social Research*. London: Unwin Hyman/Routledge.

Charmaz, K. (1990) 'Discovering chronic illness: using grounded theory', *Social Science and Medicine*, 30: 1161–72.

Charmaz, K. and Mitchell, R.G. (2001) 'Grounded theory in ethnography', in P. Atkinson, A. Coffey, S. Delamont, J. Lofland and L. Lofland (eds), *Handbook of Ethnography*. London: Sage, pp. 160–74.

Charmaz, K. (2003) 'Grounded theory', in J.A. Smith (ed.), *Qualitative Psychology: A Practical Guide to Research Methods*. London: Sage, pp. 81–110.

Charmaz, K. (2006) *Constructing Grounded Theory: A Practical Guide Through Qualitative Analysis*. London: Sage.

Coffey, A. and Atkinson, P. (1996) *Making Sense of Qualitative Data Analysis: Complementary Research Strategies*. London: Sage.

Crotty, M. (1998) *The Foundations of Social Research: Meaning and Perspective in the Research Process*. London: Sage.

Cryer, P. (2000) *The Research Student's Guide to Success*. Buckingham: Open University Press.

Daiute, C. and Lightfoot, C. (eds) (2004) *Narrative Analysis: Studying the Development of Individuals in Society*. Thousand Oaks, CA: Sage.

Delamont, S., Atkinson, P. and Parry, O. (1997) *Supervising the PhD: A Guide to Success*. Buckingham: The Society for Research into Higher Education and Open University Press.

Denzin, N.K. (1970) *The Research Act*. Chicago: Aldine.

Denzin, N.K. (1989) *Interpretive Interactionism*. Newbury Park, CA: Sage.

Denzin, N.K. (1997) *Interpretive Ethnography*. London: Sage.

Denzin, N.K. (2004) 'The art and politics of interpretation', in S.N. Hesse-Biber and P. Leavy (eds), *Approaches to Qualitative Research*. New York: Oxford University Press, pp. 447–72.

Denzin, N.K. and Lincoln, Y.S. (1998) 'Entering the field of qualitative research', in N.K. Denzin and Y.S. Lincoln (eds), *Strategies of Qualitative Inquiry*. London: Sage, pp.1–3A.

Dey, I. (1993) *Qualitative Data Analysis: A User-friendly Guide for Social Scientists*. London: Routledge.

Emerson, R.M., Fretz, R.I. and Shaw, L.L. (1995) *Writing Ethnographic Fieldnotes*. Chicago: University of Chicago Press.

Emerson, R.M., Fretz, R.I. and Shaw, L.L. (2001) 'Participant observation and fieldnotes', in P. Atkinson, A. Coffey, S. Delamont, J. Lofland and L. Lofland (eds), *Handbook of Ethnography*. London: Sage, pp. 352–68.

Fielding, N.G. and Lee, R.M. (1998) *Computer Analysis and Qualitative Research*. London: Sage.

Fielding, N.G. and Lee, R.M. (eds) (1991) *Using Computers in Qualitative Research*. London: Sage.

Finch, J. (1984) '"It's great to have someone to talk to" Ethics and Politics of Interviewing Women', in C. Bell and H. Roberts (eds), *Social Researching: Politics, Problems, Practice*. London: Routledge, pp. 70–87.

Flick, U. (2006) *An Introduction to Qualitative Research*. 3rd edn. London: Sage.

Flick, U. (2007a) *Designing Qualitative Research* (Book 1 of *The SAGE Qualitative Research Kit*) London: Sage.

Flick, U. (2007b) *Managing Quality in Qualitative Research* (Book 8 of *The SAGE Qualitative Research Kit*) London: Sage.

Flick, U., von Kardorff, E. and Steinke, I. (eds) (2004) *A Companion to Qualitative Research*. London: Sage.

Frank, A.W. (1995) *The Wounded Storyteller: Body, Illness and Ethics*. Chicago: The University of Chicago Press.

Geertz, C. (1975) 'Thick description: toward an interpretive theory of culture', in C. Geertz (ed.), *The Interpretation of Cultures*. London: Hutchinson, pp. 3–30.

Gibbs, G.R. (2002) *Qualitative Data Analysis: Explorations with NVivo*. Buckingham: Open University Press.

Giorgi, A. and Giorgi, B. (2003) 'Phenomenology', in J.A. Smith (ed.), *Qualitative Psychology: A Practical Guide to Research Methods*. London: Sage, pp. 25–50.

Glaser, B.G. (1978) *Theoretical Sensitivity: Advances in the Methodology of Grounded Theory*. Mill Valley, CA: Sociology Press.

Glaser, B.G. (1992) *Emergence vs Forcing: Basics of Grounded Theory Analysis*. Mill Valley, CA: Sociology Press.

Glaser, B.G. and Strauss, A.L. (1967) *The Discovery of Grounded Theory: Strategies for Qualitative Research*. Chicago: Aldine.

Gregory, D., Russell, C.K. and Phillips, L.R. (1997) 'Beyond textual perfection: transcribers as vulnerable persons', *Qualitative Health Research*, 7: 294–300.

Guba, E.G. and Lincoln, Y.S. (1989) *Fourth Generation Evaluation*. Newbury Park, CA: Sage.

Hartley, J. (1989) 'Tools for evaluating text', in J. Hartley and A. Branthwaite (eds), *The Applied Psychologist*. Milton Keynes: Open University Press.

Hesse-Biber, S.N. and Leavy, P. (eds) (2004) *Approaches to Qualitative Research. A Reader on Theory and Practice*. New York. Oxford University Press.

King, N. (1998) 'Template analysis', in G. Symon and C. Cassell (eds), *Qualitative Methods and Analysis in Organizational Research.* London: Sage.

Kvale, S. (1988) 'The 1000-page question', *Phenomenology and Pedagogy,* 6: 90–106.

Kvale, S. (1996) *InterViews: An Introduction to Qualitative Research Interviewing.* Thousand Oaks, CA: Sage.

Kvale, S. (2007) *Doing Interviews* (Book 2 of *The SAGE Qualitative Research Kit*) London: Sage.

Labov, W. (1972) 'The transformation of experience in narrative syntax', in W. Labov (ed.), *Language in the Inner City: Studies in the Black English Vernacular.* Philadelphia, PA: University of Pennsylvania Press, pp. 354–96.

Labov, W. (1982) 'Speech actions and reactions in personal narrative', in D. Tannen (ed.), *Analyzing Discourse: Text and Talk.* Washington, DC: Georgetown University Press, pp. 219–47.

Labov, W. and Waletsky, J. (1967) 'Narrative analysis: oral versions of personal experi-ence', in J. Helm (ed.), *Essays on the Verbal and Visual Arts.* Seattle, WA: University of Washington Press, pp. 12–44.

Lewins, A. and Silver, C. (2007) *Using Software in Qualitative Research: A Step-by-Step Guide.* London: Sage.

Lofland, J., Snow, D., Anderson, L. and Lofland, L.H. (2006) *Analyzing Social Settings: A Guide to Qualitative Observation and Analysis.* Belmont, CA: Wadsworth/Thomson.

McAdams, D. (1993) *The Stories We Live By: Personal Myths and the Making of the Self.* New York: Guilford Press.

Marshall, C. and Rossman, G.B. (2006) *Designing Qualitative Research* (4th edn). London: Sage.

Maso, I. (2001) 'Phenomenology and ethnography', in P. Atkinson, A. Coffey, S. Delamont, J. Lofland and L. Lofland (eds), *Handbook of Ethnograpy.* London: Sage. pp. 136–44.

Mason, J. (1996) *Qualitative researching.* London: Sage.

Mason, J. (2002) *Qualitative researching* (2nd edn). London: Sage.

Maykut, P. and Morehouse, R. (2001) *Beginning Qualitative Research: A Philosophical and Practical Guide.* London: RoutledgeFalmer.

Miles, M.B. and Huberman, A.M. (1994) *Qualitative Data Analysis: A Sourcebook of New Methods.* Beverly Hills, CA: Sage.

Mills, C.W. (1940) 'Situated actions and vocabularies of motive', *American Sociological Review,* 5(6): 439–52.

Mishler, E.G. (1986) 'The analysis of interview narratives', in T.R. Sarbin (ed.), *Narrative Psychology.* New York: Praeger, pp. 233–55.

Mishler, E.G. (1991) 'Representing discourse: the rhetoric of transcription', *Journal of Narrative and Life History,* 1: 255–80.

Moustakas, C. (1994) *Phenomenological Research Methods.* Thousand Oaks, CA: Sage.

Park, J. and Zeanah, A. (2005) 'An evaluation of voice recognition software for use in interview-based research: a research note', *Qualitative Reasearch,* 5(2): 245–51.

Plummer, K. (2001) *Documents of Life 2: An Invitation to a Critical Humanism.* London: Sage.

Poland, B.D. (2001) 'Transcription Quality', in J.F. Gubrium and J.A. Holstein (eds), *Handbook of Interview Research: Context and Method.* Thousand Oaks, CA: Sage, pp. 629–49.

Rapley, T. (2007) *Doing Conversation, Discourse and Document Analysis* (Book 7 of *The SAGE Qualitative Research Kit*). London: Sage.

Richardson, L. (2004) 'Writing: a method of inquiry', in S.N. Hesse-Biber and P. Leavy (eds), *Approaches to Qualitative Research. A Reader on Theory and Practice.* New York: Oxford University Press, pp. 473–95.

Ricoeur, P. (1984) *Time and Narrative*, trans. K. McLaughlin and D. Pellauer. Chicago: University of Chicago Press.

Riessman, C.K. (1993) *Narrative Analysis*. Newbury Park, CA: Sage.

Ritchie, J. and Lewis, J. (eds) (2003) *Qualitative Research Practice: A Guide for Social Science Students and Researchers*. London: Sage.

Ritchie, J., Spencer, L. and O'Connor, W. (2003) 'Carrying out qualitative analysis', in J. Ritchie and J. Lewis (eds), *Qualitative Research Practice: A Guide for Social Science Students and Researchers*. London: Sage, pp. 219–62.

Ryen, A. (2004) 'Ethical issues', in C.F. Seale, G. Gobo, J.F. Gubrium and D. Silverman (eds), *Qualitative Research Practice*. London: Sage, pp. 230–47.

Seale, C.F. (1999) *The Quality of Qualitative Research*. London: Sage.

Seale, C.F. (2001) 'Computer-assisted analysis of qualitative interview data', in J.F. Gubrium and J.A. Holstein (eds), *Handbook of Interview Research: Context and Method*. Thousand Oaks, CA: Sage, pp. 651–70.

Seale, C.F. (2002) 'Cancer heroics: a study of news reports with particular reference to gender', *Sociology*, 36: 107–26.

Silverman, D. (ed.) (1997) *Qualitative Research: Theory, Method and Practice*. London: Sage.

Smith, J.A. (1995) 'Semi-structured interview and qualitative analysis', in J.A. Smith, R. Harré and L. van Langenhove (eds), *Rethinking Methods in Psychology*. London: Sage, pp. 9–26.

Strauss, A.L. (1987) *Qualitative Analysis for Social Scientists*. Cambridge: Cambridge University Press.

Strauss, A.L. and Corbin, J. (1990) *Basics of Qualitative Research, Grounded Theory Procedures and Techniques*. Thousand Oaks, CA: Sage.

Strauss, A.L. and Corbin, J. (1997) *Grounded Theory in Practice*. London: Sage.

Strauss, A.L. and Corbin, J. (1998) *Basics of Qualitative Research: Techniques and Procedures for developing Grounded Theory* (2nd edn). Thousand Oaks, CA: Sage.

Van Maanen, J. (1988) *Tales of the Field: On Writing Ethnography*. Chicago: University of Chicago Press.

Weaver, A. and Atkinson, P. (1994) *Microcomputing and Qualitative Data Analysis*. Aldershot: Avebury.

Wolcott, H.F. (2001) *Writing Up Qualitative Research* (2nd edn). Newbury Park, CA: Sage.

▌▌▌ Author index

‖ Subject index